VERSE, RHYME
&
OCCASIONAL REASON

(Occasional Verse for Some
Reasonable Occasions)

**A sample of Forty Years of Versification
"Some Diversify, Some just Versify!"**

*May the poetic mosaic
Outlive the linear prosaic.*

A. George Fells

i

VERSE, RHYME AND OCCASIONAL REASON

Library and Archives Canada Cataloguing in Publication

Fells, A. George
Verse, rhyme & occasional reason: occasional verse for some reasonable occasions : a sample of forty years of versification, "some diversify, some just versify!" / A. George Fells.

ISBN 978-0-9737545-8-2

I. Title.

PS8611.E464V47 2007
C811'.6   C2007-905893-0

Includes index.
ISBN 978-0-9737545-8-2

This edition published in 2007 by Cybercom Publishing
PO Box 130, Dorset, Ontario Canada P0A 1E0

Email: cybercompublishing@gmail.com

Edited by: Sheila Pennington Ph.D.
Cover, layout and text design: Tim Harrison
Cover illustration: A. George Fells
Interior illustrations: Chapters I-111 and V1, A. George Fells
Chapters IV, V, and VII-IX, Anthony Jenkins

Printed and bound in the United States of America and
England.

ABOUT THE AUTHOR

George Fells was born in 1933 in Clifton, England. Following the outbreak of World War II his father was sent overseas with the army and George and his mother moved to a cottage in rural Buckinghamshire. He attended St. Louis preparatory school in Banbury and then St. Edwards in Oxford.

Following the completion of his National Service with the Durham Light Infantry as an officer in the British Commonwealth Forces in Korea and Japan, he returned to Corpus Christi College, Oxford where he earned his M.A. in English.

In 1956 he emigrated to Canada, spent several years in market research and real estate development, then joined the venture capital firm of Charterhouse Canada. Subsequently he was a founder of S B Capital Corporation and North American Ventures Fund. He retired in 1993 and continues to live with his wife Kittie in Toronto, on his farm in Mono Township, Ontario and his Georgian Bay island retreat. They have two children and three grandchildren.

Throughout his life, George has combined action with commentary. While managing two companies, he lectured extensively in Canada and internationally; served on numerous boards of directors; produced a Home Study course for business owner-managers and wrote numerous articles on business topics as well as a variety of more esoteric subjects. He has written poetry; some formal, some celebratory, some highly introspective. It is a selection of these works that are presented here.

OPINIONS OF OTHERS

VERSE, RHYME AND OCCASIONAL REASON

Part VII– The Business of Business

Part VIII – In Memoriam

Part IX – One (and two) Liners

DEDICATION

To my long suffering wife, Kittie; my children, Emily and Duncan; my son-in-law, Ghislain; grandchildren, Mathieu, Marie-Claire and Genevieve; to Mary Sargent, my thorough and dedicated secretary whose sense of humour is always at hand; and to all those people, events, memories and experiences which give rise to occasional flights of fancy and imagination, too often missing in a world of frantic action.

FOREWORD

It was Dr. Johnson who said, "Occasional verse must expect only occasional praise." And that surely is all I expect, as well perhaps as a laugh or a tear or an occasional jog of memory. I certainly don't ask for more.

Having since childhood loved words – their sounds, their meanings, their innuendos, their rhythms, their capacity to prompt flights of fancy and evoke memories of the real and the imagined – I have over the years jotted down some, but far from all, of my musings. Having been brought up on John Donne, Blake, Wordsworth, Tennyson and the like, I eschew the wandering, unrhymed and non-rhythmic lines that wander across the page in much of modern poetry.

The reader will soon find that I prefer rhythm, end-rhymes and the scanning metre that is so often absent in today's verse. May it bring back fond memories.

Occasionally, as is fit perhaps for occasional verse, some pieces have been previously published, like Acer Negundo, The Motive and a few others. Many, but not all, both published and unpublished, are offered here for my own memory's sake; for my children and close family; and for others who like to look in dark closets and forgotten corners to uncover and, perhaps, recover the past.

DEAD CEDARS.

A97
SEPT 5 '98

Part I – Travel & Nature

Scarista House

We sit with sombre face,
We talk in muted tone
We raise our glance
Upon the chance
A voice exceeds a drone.

We munch our salted kippers,
Our Scottish porridge sip;
And roll our oats
Down tightened throats,
With stiffened upper lip.

We walk the rugged moors
With measured British stride.
We brace our knees
Against the breeze
With stiffened English pride.

We dress ourselves for dinner,
Choose wine to suit the course.
From soup to meat,
From cheese to sweet,
Each one a tour de force.

We sign a hefty cheque.
We make our move to go;
With hearty shake,
Our leave we take;
"It was a splendid show."

Summer of '84

We signed up with Martin Lewis
For Biology Three Thousand 0-Three
For three weeks of High Arctic tundra
No sight of a familiar tree.

So we sorted out long underwear
While sweltering in dry southern heat;
Six pairs of heavy wool socks
Kodiaks and Wellies for feet.

> *Oh, we signed up with Martin Lewis*
> *For Biology Three Thousand 0-Three*
> *For ten miles of hard walks each day*
> *And a primer in botany.*

No need for your old bathing suit
Or a flashlight for use at night,
Or a compass for finding your way
If you don't know your left from your right.

Up there its perpetual day
In the summer of the Eskimo;
And at latitude 69
A compass in circles will go.

> *Oh, we signed up with Martin Lewis*
> *For Biology Three Thousand 0-Three*
> *Just bring your own hammer and spanner*
> *For there's work to do as you'll see.*

There's garbage from the old DEW line;
There're generators heavy and mean;
And Martin would be damned if he didn't
Remove the whole lot from the scene.

"An experience you'll never forget"
Were his words to describe the affair;
When we arrived at the Sarpca airstrip
There was a menacing threat in the air.

> *Oh, we signed up with Martin Lewis*
> *For Biology Three Thousand 0-Three*
> *For two weeks of gale-like wind*
> *And one helluva clean-up spree.*

If the smell of a honey bucket
Will turn up your delicate nose;
Or washing your clothes in a kettle,
Or yourself under trickling hose.

Then stay back down in the South,
And miss a spectacular thrill.
What's a worn-out duffle or glove,
Some oil or honey pail spill?

> *Oh, we signed up with Martin Lewis*
> *For Biology Three ThousandThree*
> *And learned a lot about clean-up*
> *And even some biology.*

We dismantled generators
We put up sixty-foot towers;

We hardly thought of our projects
As we played in the midnight hours.

There was Nancy, Cathy and Grace;
Cindy and Michelle made a pair;
Then Michelle made a play for Carey
And you'd think there was no one else there.

Tony had been there before,
And Don was the camp's medico;
Nancy looked after Ferns
And George was just rearing to go.

Kittie was resident artist,
And Duncan looked after the food;
Mike was good at just anything,
We all kept in a pretty good mood.

At least we now know the difference
Between a Draba and a purple Braya
And that the bract on a Carex Stans
Than the seed grows somewhat higher.

If to you Pedicula is ridiculous,
And Lesquerella is no more than a dance,
You should sign up with Martin Lewis
And give yourself just one more chance.

Oh, we signed up with Martin Lewis
For Biology Three Thousand 0-Three
And now we all know Leguminosa
Is only the name of a pea.

From Sarpca we came out early
To be sure to catch the next flight;
It took some negotiating
To find us a place for the night.

But it all worked out in the end
As the Bay opened up its door,
And we took over the junior school
And Duncan had one final snore.

Next day it was off to Frobisher
Back down to the land of the heat;
To green trees, cars and people
And hard concrete under our feet.

And we all looked back with joy
At the marvellous times we had had;
And hoped we'd soon meet again
To recall the good and the bad.

Like the wind that blew in at Sarpca
And Cathy's warm rock in the sun,
The frigid updraft in the outhouse!
Each twenty-four hours filled with fun.

Oh, we signed up with Martin Lewis
For Biology Three Thousand 0-Three
And had the best time in our life.
Even learned some Biology!

Song of Quetico

Quetico, Quetico,
That's the place we love to go

Nine thousand years of history
Untold years of mystery
It's painted on the rocky walls
It echoes in the wildlife calls
Let's treat it with respect and care
Leave no sign that we've been there.

Look west of the roaring Great Lakes,
Look north where the Thunder Head breaks,
Where Native and Voyageur met
The course of our destiny set.
In the wildness of Quetico find
Fresh strength for body and mind.

In Saganaga or Basswood Lakes
The Voyageurs knew what it takes
To get their furs from northern forts
Far down east to the waiting ports.
They swung their paddles strong and free
Along the route of La Verendrey.

The trout and bass in waters pure
Are watchful for the casting lure;
Wolf and moose their trails do take
In dappled shadows by the lake,

Where the hermit thrush sings evensong
In the twilight still and long.
Let's put ashore and find a site

Set-up camp for the coming night,
Where the waves are dancing with the moon
And the shores are echoing to the loon;
Where the nights are silent and still
Caressed by the white-throat's trill.

Where the proud Ojibwa band
Still cross their ancestral land;
Pictographs recount the past
To keep traditions strong and fast;
Where Elders keep their memories true
In respect of Manitou.

Through names like Wagwagun
Deux Revieres and Ferguson
Catch the spirit of the place,
Read man's sad history in its face.
Then swear to God or Manitou,
"Let nature be to nature true."

Nine thousand years of history,
Untold years of mystery;
It's painted on the rocky walls,
It echoes in the wildlife calls.
Let's treat it with respect and care,
Leave no sign that we've been there.

Quetico, Quetico
That's the place we love to go.

Acer Negundo or Lowly Manitoba Maple

Not tall, not graceful
But craggy, rough and strong
In nature's way.
They criticise my skin,
Which flakes, they say.
My limbs too knotted, twisted
Not useful for their ways,
Uneconomic.
Soft, they say, to the core.

But ask the birds
That thrilled me with their feet
Or pecked my bark for food to eat;
From my torso and my arms
Tore tasty strips;
Or roosted there o'ernight
Protected from the owl that prowls
Whose ghostly voice sent shivers
Down their spines;
Made feathers ruffle, heads on shoulders sink
Buried in muffled fear of night's assault,
That I could shield them from.

And yet those others
Pronounced me dirty, useless
Because I shed a tear of bark
Or tassled florets in the spring.
What right have they to say
"Cut it down, it's no good
It's a weed,
It's a useless bit of wood!"

For boards they cannot use me
Or batten, slat or cupboard;
My sawdust, chips or twigs,
Leaves or bark have no use
For them; "Cut it down, clean it up,
Pretend it never lived," they said.

But now I'm dead, and now I'm gone
Just listen to the songs of sorrow
When chickadee, nut-hatch, wood-pecker,
Blue Jay, sparrows of every ilk
Circle where once I stood
Arms outstretched, haven of branches
For those who ask for nothing
But to be left alone.

Now nothing's left
But sighs of empty air.
No place to hide, no perch,
No refuge there.

Sic homines sunt;
Thus are men.
Won't they ever learn?

Ozzie Land

You know you're in Australia
The land of the 'Roo;
The gum and the Koala
And the Pink Cockatoo …

If a wave's pronounced "wive"
And a mate is a "mite"
If a ranch is a "station";
They don't drive on the right.

If door handles are high
And the John flushes two;
A half for a widdle
And a full for a "poo".

>   "Yes,
>   *You know you're in the land of the 'Roo*
>   *The gum and Koala and the Pink Cockatoo."*

If a girl's called a "Sheila";
An outhouse a "dunny";
A beer is a "stubby";
And rugby's played funny.

If a hat's called a "Slouch"
If a "dingo's" a dog;
If garbage is rubbish
And booze is called "grog.

"Yes,
You know you're in the land of the 'Roo
The gum and Koala and the Pink Cockatoo."

If the galas scream murder
At the end of the day;
If "Gooday" is the greeting
As you pass on your way,

If Victoria's Bitter
Is known as V.B.
If a cyclone's a "blow"
A beer can a "tinny"

   "Yes,
   You know you're in the land of the 'Roo
   The gum and Koala and the Pink Cockatoo."

If mosquitoes are "mossies"
When they swarm in your camp;
If what's known as "bushwack"
Is to trek or to tramp

If "Good-on-ye" means
"Good, you did well"
If a "shout" buys a round
If being "crook" is not well …

   "Yes,
   You know you're in the land of the 'Roo
   The gum and Koala and the Pink Cockatoo."

Bathurst Inlet Lodge
(July 7 – 14, 1996)

For you, you happy campers,
Who enjoyed this Arctic treasure,
I offer up these verses
In fake iambic measure.

We came to Bathurst Inlet
The Arctic to explore
To see the flowers and wildlife
And life along the shore.

We found what we had come for
In plentiful profusion;
Though places and the faces
Gave room for much confusion.

There was Robert, John and Connie
There was Sam and Allen too
And George and brother Tommy
With Susie in the crew.

With Jessie, Martha, Bella
And Karen on the go
Helping Glen and Travis
And Trish keep up the show.

There was food and drink aplenty;
A self-service "honour" bar.
And tea and coffee-creamer
Always ready in a jar.

Then there were "resources"
And what wonders they would prove;
The Bishop of the Arctic
Whose words you should behoove.

He told us of his people
Of the language that they speak,
Of their customs and beliefs;
The traditions that they keep.

Then Page from Cincinnati,
Took on all the rest;
From geology to fauna,
And the flora she loved best.

She led us up the beaches,
As our naturalist supreme;
She showed us glaciers plucking
From a rock of smoothest sheen.

She led us up to ridges
Along faults quite sedimentary;
She showed us quartzite riches
In geologic elementary.

She also showed us flora
Of every type and hue;
From the taller growing Alder,
To anemones of blue.

Funguses and algae
In relations symbiotic

That formed the bed for others;
To start colonies exotic.

There were Carexes or sedges
Eriophorum by the score;
Cotton grasses single,
And double by the shore.

Lilies named Puscilla
Orchids Chlorophyllous;
And Carex Membranaceous
And even Aquatilus.

Then there were the pea types,
Leguminosa all;
Richardson, Lupinus
And Oxytropa tall.

There's also Potentilla
Some know as Cinquefoil;
And Saxifrages many;
To list is too much toil.

Just remember your Nivalis
Triscuspidata too.
And Stellarius on its tap-root
And she'll be proud of you.

In English its much simpler;
Alpine, Nodding, Brook
And Marsh and Mountain Yellow -
It's all Page's book!

And buttercups, anemones,
Some with a wash of blue;
Drabex, Alpine and Nivalis
To drop a name or two!

Then there are the willows
In numbers quite ridiculous.
There's Richardson's and Arctic
And one called "Reticulatus".

But what to Page is simple,
To us is great confusion
As the so-called "barren" arctic
Yielded species in profusion.

Now the animals were simpler
As they numbered only few.
A grizzly and ground squirrels,
And some scattered caribou.

But still we scan the skyline
For the elusive Musken ox,
And look behind each outcrop
For the silken Arctic fox.

As for birds, there's plenty;
Just scan the arctic sky
Loons, red-necked and yellow bill;
Golden eagles flying high.

There's sparrows, tree and white crowned,
And the beautiful Savannah.
There's Phalaropes and Longspurs …
For birders, its Nirvana!

For you, you happy campers
Who enjoyed this Arctic treasure,
I've offered up these verses
In fake iambic measure.

Yes, we thank our host and hostess
Glen, Trish and helpers all.
To beat this great experience,
Would be an order tall!

Nahanni River Adventure
Rob and His Crew
(June 30 – July 7, 1996)

If you can't stand the rip of a sliding zip
Or a tent in the midnight sun;
If a yell from the stern gives your stomach a turn
As you start on a rapid's run;
If the spray on your head or the sand in your bed
Makes you wish you had never come …

Refrain

Then you're not for Rob and his crew
For Peter the Redhead or Ben with his curls
With their knots, and their pots and their acrobat
twirls,
And their gourmet delights and feats of white
knights.
No, you're not for Rob and his crew.

If you're late for your flight and the airline's uptight
When you crash the departure gate;

If the bear noise next door is only a snore
From the guy who was nearly late;
If the stroke of the paddle makes too much of a
struggle
To keep up with this rollicking rate …

If the river's too strong and the days are too long
As you set out on this northern trip;
If wildness is quiet and fast food is your diet
And you'd prefer a coke for a nip;
If a sulphurous smell makes you think you're in hell
And the hot springs are not for your dip …
If the torrents of rain make your spirits to wane
In the Splits on the way to the Butte;
If spotting a mouse, three lambs and a grouse
Make you regret just leaving your house…..

Refrain

Then you're not for Rob and his crew
For Peter the Redhead or Ben with his curls
With their knots, and their pots and their acrobat
twirls,
And their gourmet delights and feats of white
knights.
No, you're not for Rob and his crew.

If you think its just fate to have holes in your plate
There's not a thing on this trip you will hate …
If your paddle is steady approaching an eddy,
Then for fun on the rocks you are ready;
If you want nice guys as your Big River guides
To find what the Nahanni still hides …
Then you're just right for Rob and his crew.

31

Refrain

> Then you're not for Rob and his crew
> For Peter the Redhead or Ben with his curls
> With their knots, and their pots and their acrobat
> twirls,
> And their gourmet delights and feats of white
> knights.
> Yes, you're right for Rob and his crew.

With help from fellow travellers – July '96
KAREN and GARY MARTIN,
ALLAN HIRSH and PETER SEVITT,
and ROBERT HARPER

Cruising the Isis Without Crisis

> A narrow boat
> Will stay afloat
> Who'ere the rotten skipper.
>
> But woe-betide
> Those caught inside,
> Not on deck and chipper!

Table Rock

What better place to spread
    Our picnic on the rock,
To pop the cork, and cut the bread
    Than fabled, Table Rock?

It was September on the Bay
    The "tourists" all departed;
No wind no, rain, a perfect day
    And we content, ligh-hearted.

We marvelled at Bill Grierson,
    The haven he's created
'gainst the elements most fearsome
    Where nature's wrath is sated.

Bill, you really shouldn't leave it
    In the calmness of September;
These shortening days, believe it,
    Are the best ones to remember.

In peace and new found vigour
    We leave your tranquil isle
Prepared to face Fall's rigour
    With a warm and thankful smile.

A Better Mousetrap ?

Back broken, not
In work or play
Nor pursuit
Of pleasure
But of food
Life's imperative.

Eyes bulging
Nose bleeding
Feet still clenched
On thin air.

Don't tell me
We can't build
A better mousetrap.

Spring

The air is soft and gentle now
The storms of winter gone
And in their place a warming breeze
Lifts wings on rays of sun.

The swallows soar in courtship's dance;
Crows mob a tiresome hawk.
Finches, sparrows, chickadees
Exchange their spring-time talk.

Dull brown is gently stroked with green,
Drab winter giving way
To spring-time's endless cries of joy
To greet the lengthening day.

Part II – Philosophical

Overwhelmed

I wake up full of rhyme,
Which lasts through breakfast-time.
But then the world in trouble
Explodes my selfish bubble.
Filled with gloom by noon,
A hostage in my room.
Then overwhelmed with sadness
At man's compulsive madness,
I survey the world's mosaic,
And revert to the prosaic.
Slip down beneath the covers …
Leave these problems to the others.

The Dye is Caste

The dye is caste
The stone is thrown
The ripple washes outward.

The hour will pass
The hand will turn
With no one glancing backwards.

Blood Letting

A little dose of letting blood
Was never seen as bad;
In fact it was medicinal
The only cure they had.

Panic Mode

Is it panic mode
Or manic mood?
It matters not a jot.

It clouds the sun
Wipes out the fun
Leaves me a sulking clot.

Alternative to the U.S. Dream

When the husband chops wood
  And the wife bakes the bread
You can bet George Bush
  Has gone right out of his head.

Who needs World's Free Trade
  Or large trading blocks
Or Roots for your feet
  When you can still darn your socks.

If perpetual consumption
  Is the answer you like
Then I'm opting out.
  Let Bush take a hike.

I'd rather be happy
  With a smile on my face
Than wake up in the morning
  To join the rat-race.

We'll keep our clothes longer
  We'll bake our own bread;
We'll keep our jalopy
  And our falling down shed.

We'll grow our own veggies
  Trade beans for a steak;
For fences have hedges,
  Our own jams we will make.

We'll consume a lot less
  Make really no waste
No packaging mess
  To preserve a false taste.

We'll suffer no dearth
  More soundly we'll sleep;
While reducing our girth
  To ourselves will we keep

A Response to Weird and Wonderful Words

I jiffle[1] here amid the rocks
Send you metaphoric hongi[2]
There's a hummer florisugent[3]
At my window looking hungry.

---

1 Fidget
2 Madri Greeting
3 Sucking honey from a flower

There's a river discomboquing[4]
From the rocks across the slew[5]
I swear I am not joking,
'cause they'll sometimes catch a plew[6]

Tonight we'll have for dinner
A plate of bubbling speck[7]
Dessert for an aging sinner
No venison or elk!

At times I cause myself to squirk[8]
When in moments most solein[9]
In vain I try to vaticinate[10]
But the future's never plain.

So 'ere I stare a steracle[11]
Or become an aging stogey[12]
'Ere for ignorance crapulous[13]
They put me out on pogey,[14]

Its now, my dearest niefling,[15]

---

4 Pouring out
5 Pond (not in book) also Slough
6 Beaver
7 A dish of onions and mashed potatoes
  with a large lump of butter or lard in the middle
8 A half suppressed laugh
9 Done alone or in privacy
10 Predict events
11 A spectacle or show
12 Like a cigar (not in book)
13 Related to alcohol or drunkenness
14 Welfare (I think – not in book)
15 Nephew or niece – take your pick!

In style most autocogical[16]
I'll exit from my speechling
In a style I'll call Kenspeckle[17]

So 'ere another steracle [18]
Of ignorance sublime
I'll draw in sand chimerical[19]
A planeticosal line![20]

Thanks for the endless digression
May it not induce obsession.
With help from my relative Ben Barnes

Take It From Me

I can't tell you how,
I can't tell you why
But I know what's hot
And I know what's not.
As a general rule
I know what's cool.

If you think it's in
To commit a sin
With your best friend's girl
You're a rat, a churl.
If you think its cool

---

16 Adjective with the proper noun it describes – figure that one!
17 Scottish meaning "conspicuous, easily recognizable"
18 As above-spectacle or show
19 Imaginary
20 Liking to wander

To cheat at pool;
Or tell a lie
To explain just why
You took Dad's car
To the local bar;
Or took that cash
From his secret stash
He keeps on hand
To help, be kind
To guys at the door
Who want one more
Dime for a coke.
Its not a joke

Yes, I know what's hot
And I know what's not.

Heather in the Outhouse

When Heather was visiting the Fells
  On their island on Georgian Bay
There's a story her sister still tells
  Of one embarrassing day!

When Heather just needed to "go"
  To the outhouse she sensibly went.
But what Heather hadn't reason to know
  Was the strength of the wind through the vent.

As soon as she'd sat herself down
  Then the wind on the door gave a blow,
And even before she could frown
  The latch shifted into "no go".

If it wasn't for Laura her sister
  Who noticed her time spent away
And was just beginning to miss her,
  It might have turned out a bad day.

Out went a search party of one
  To rescue the missing young Heather;
And found her there locked in the John
  The victim of blustery weather.

A few tears of frustration were shed
  But more she was angry and mad,
As young Heather was thankfully led
  To the arms of her Mummy and Dad.

Just One of Those Days

Is it just one of those days?
The alarm didn't ding
The phone had to ring
Is it just me that gets treated this way?

Is it just one of those days?
The toast got burned black
My plate had a crack
The milk's all gone sour
Missed the train by an hour
Is it just me that gets treated this way?

Is it just one of those days?
I'm given to wonder
Is it really God's thunder

That's singled me out
Given me a good clout
On both of my ears
To drive me to tears?
Is it just me that gets treated this way?

Is it me that gets treated this way?
If I got it all wrong
Please ding the old gong;
I made a mistake
Just give me a break
I take it all back
Don't give me the rack
I'll stand in the corner
Like Little Jack Horner
Is it just me that gets treated this way?

Is it just one of those days?
Just tell me its so
Don't let the world know
I'll go back to bed
I'll cover my head
Pull blankets up high
Won't look at the sky
Pretend I'm not there
At the ceiling I'll stare
Bury my sorrow
And pretend it's not me you treated this way.

Just say it's a deal
Then better I'll feel
Oh, it just has to be one of those days.

"Border Banter"
A Serious Response to a Light-Hearted Complaint

While your rhyme does surely have its rhythm
   It falls short, perhaps, by way of reason,
We northern folk have that queasy feeling
   That on us its always open season!

What with Cuba and your interference
   And attempts to dominate our culture,
Try to understand, your U.S. eagle
   Seems more to us like venal vulture.

Now to you dear cousin we will admit
   That we do lack a certain confidence;
Just bickering with our southern neighbour
   Displays our self-destructing diffidence.

But having to that with grace admitted
   Let's tell you straight, make no mistake
Your nation's gall, conceit and righteousness
   Give others and us too, a belly-ache.

Have you forgotten history's lessons?
   The rise and fall of principality?
The sway of power, the pendulum's swing?
   That pride precedes a lost morality?

Our beef with you is not that attorneys
   To us are known by the humbler name
Of lawyers; that route to us is rhymed with root;
   Our garbage to your trash is just the same.

No, 'tis that you recognize no others
  Nor other ways to tread this earthly path;
To organize a nation's people
  Appease God and nature's waiting wrath.

We too have our pride; a mixing pot,
  And multi-culture is where we're aimed.
Our freedom to speak is ever present
  But in tones less strident, yes more restrained.

Till such time as the tables choose to turn,
  The Orient raising its powerful, wakening head,
Let us carp and gripe, at our neighbours snipe.
  Would you rather our politics turned red?

To The Importunate Lover

It's unfortunate
You're importunate;
Your bold advances
Reduce your chances
Of satisfaction
Yes, only gratification
Is your lover's aim.
Your loss is my gain.

The Bored Sophomore

I'm a soporific sophomore;
Getting out of bed is quite a chore;
I don't go to lectures any more;
Oh, my life is such a dreadful bore.

Foot in Mouth

When foot is put in mouth
Or tongue is put in cheek
It's amazing what results you get
From young or old, or bold or meek.

Routine Revisited

There's much to be said for routine,
    Provided its occasionally broken,
Leaving time for surprise and invention
    And feelings that need to be spoken.

The Happy Broker

Neither bull nor bear
Will see me here
I'll be out just spending money.

Stocks go up, bonds go down;
The Markets smile or frown.
I'll go spend it on my honey.

I need no permission
To spend my commission
Just clients to buy or sell.

If you lose or gain
I'll feel no pain
High water or dogs of hell!

So let the bulls keep on roaring
And the markets keep soaring
I'll ride them all like a bronco.

And if the Bears start a groaning
And investors start moaning
I'll be out of here, but pronto

George's Writing

George, old boy, you really should learn
    To write with a hand that is rounded and firm.
Get rid of the cramp and restrictions
    Let the reader read fact not just fiction.

Sign on the Message Box

I'm a lonely little box on the wall
Doing nothing much useful at all.
It would make me feel better
If you'd drop in a letter.
Legible, please, not a scrawl.

Three Little Keys
(for the grandchildren)

There were three little keys
All held on a chain
Who lived in dark places
In sunshine or rain.

In purses, in wallets,
In dusty dark drawers,

In cases, in satchels,
Outside and indoors.

The one for the front door
Felt he was the best …
If you couldn't get in
There'd be no place to rest.

But another bright key
With black on its top
Had control of a car;
Made it start, made it stop.

So this one thought he
Was king of the pack.
With him you got there,
With him you got back.

But a third little key
Thought she was Queen Pin
'cause the car she controlled
Was little and thin.

It would park anywhere
Could turn on a dime
And used little gas.
It worked every time.

Now the three little keys
Got along really well
And they talked about things
Just no one could tell.

They knew they controlled
The family's fate
When one day their loss
Caused a chaoticy state.

The Gra-Pa of the family
Was away on a trip
When he dropped that key-ring
… What a terrible slip!

He searched with the family
They were all on their knees
They searched every corner
Like a hive of keen bees.

There was Mummy, Gra-Pa,
Genevieve and McClaire,
Mathieu the oldest
And Daddy was there.

They looked in the cupboards
And under the stair;
They raked up the leaves,
But nothing was there.

And under the table
And under the rug;
They turned back the bedclothes
And gave them a tug.

And during this time
The keys they just giggled;
They knew they were needed …
They froze, never wriggled!

The search it went on
Through daytime and night.
They searched every corner.
It was quite a mad sight.

Then almost by chance
The Mother looked down
And there by the bureau
That key ring was found!

There were sighs of relief
And cries of delight;
It had been a long day
And a very long night.

But the keys made their point
Not inconsequential
Their role in our lives
Is always essential.

So don't take them for granted,
But treat them with care.
Then faithful and waiting,
They'll always be there.

The Protestant Ethic

If the walls of a privy that were grim
  Gave birth to original sin
Think how the rocks of the Bay
  Would have moved Martin Luther today.

In the biffy he could now contemplate
  Mankind's primordial state.
It would not take him long to see
  What the world was meant to be.

A place of beauty and grace
  With a smile on every face;
No place for the glum to be sad
  But for all to be cheerful and glad.

And by the time that his bowels had moved
  To himself he would surely have proved
That the puritan vision satanic
  Should go the way of matters organic!

Advice for the Unnamed

Ditch the bitch
Go back to Jan
You may be rich

But be a man
A vow by you
Should be always true.

Go Johnny … Go Away

My husband's a bit of a twit
Unfortunately also a wit
Which makes it not better
In fact makes it worse
Hence I'll write him this letter
That's meant as a curse.

Ode to the Old School Tie

The ties that bind
The bonds that hold
The loyalties pledged
The stories told.

The days grew long
In the heat of youth
As we set our course
In the search for truth.

The days grew long
The nights were longer
But we kept our troth
Our resolve grew stronger.

And when we'd glance
Over aching shoulder,
Or tripped by chance
On an unseen boulder.

We'd sometimes wonder
If it was all worthwhile;

We'd sometimes ponder
In the home stretch mile.

And then we'd think
With joy and pride
Of things well done
And those we'd tried.

And then we knew
It was all worthwhile;
We'd earned much pride
And a warming smile.

Thank you Teddys
For those early days;
They showed us courage
And earned us praise.

"Out of Tune"
A Villanelle

I love the mornings but they're out of tune
With the rhythm of my other half;
Her day starts at ten, mine's done by noon.

Fresh shave, push-ups and a spritely groom
Round the block to grab the morning news;
I love my mornings but they're out of tune.

Orange juice, coffee stirred with shining spoon
Toast well done with liberal marmalade;
Her day starts at ten, mine's done by noon.

Ready to face the day I reach my room
But she is on the landing, bright, waiting;
Her day starts at ten, mine's done by noon.

We compromise, downstairs we're chatting soon;
Who does what and when, but it's now past ten;
I love my mornings but they're out of tune.

So we make the most of time till noon
But time flies by and is gone too soon;
Her day starts at ten, mine's done by noon;
I love my mornings, but they're out of tune.

Advice to Bush
"Bomb Them with Butter Tarts"

Bomb them with buttertarts;
   There is no just dessert
For anger's taut frustration
   When dignity is hurt.

Bush-whack with cruise missiles
   Appease with peanut spread.
But the latter won't win smiles;
   While gunners count the dead.

If World Trade's long shadow
   Ignores another's culture
Your eagle's crackling salvo
   Won't crush their angry vulture.

Better stop the flaunting
   Of riches and your greed;

Tone down the image taunting
   Let them define their need.

Better inch toward isolation;
   Your successes seek to hide;
Try to ease their just frustration;
   Leave *them* to preen *their* pride.

My Computer

I love you computer
For your speed and your power
Your memory so agile
Saves me many an hour.

But how I do hate you
When you just won't obey
My simplest command
To do what I say.

Frustration and anger
Stretch taught my control,
When you shift, enter and delete
My hi-technical role.

All In A Lather

Oh what a bother
I'm all in a lather
Knowing not what to do.

Perhaps I had better
Compose a long letter
And sent it to God knows who!

Age's Melancholy

If old age is a second childhood
No wonder I have changed.
Those days of wandering slingshot in hand
Searching for a rabbit
Or outraged magpie,
Perhaps a startled stoat
A pheasant or duck afloat
On some shaded pond
Have gone.

Now it's hours of household chores
That take eternity, so there's never time
To contemplate
Explore hedgerows where memories lie;
A forgotten kiss or squeeze of hand
That still send shivers down the spine.

For what does the heart ache?
A second chance? Those "if only's …"
Hung on a study wall or in a diary
Stacked among those letters sent,
Received, filed but only part forgotten.

But then I had a motto once:
Never say "If I had only …"
Deeds done that did not work
Are better far than those dark holes
Of regret; better those just to forget.
"If I …"

The Canadian Dream

We do talk funny
But we stand quite proud;
We don't worship money
And we don't talk loud.

They call us Canucks;
We're a bit like the Yanks
But if you think we're the same
No way! No Thanks!

They call us cousins
And that's okay;
But we're not kissing cousins
Oh No! No Way!

The world is theirs
Or so they think.
They own it all
Dyed in deep red ink.
We're a bit more modest,
At times quite shy;
We could be tougher
If we'd only try.

As the world's safe haven,
We think we're great.
With our heads in the sand,
We'll learn too late.

By then we'll have lost it,
That Canadian dream,
There'll be no one else
But ourselves to blame.

Phone vs. Email
(To Cousin Mary)

Hi, Cousin Mary
Of Binghamton Town.
We searched for a missive
But none could be found,
Except little short notes
By some marketing grouch
And what fun you were having
On your newly bought couch.

Conversing by E-mail
I find somewhat iffy.
Touch keys and a mouse
And its off in a jiffy.
I'm stuck in a groove
With my paper and pen
Though I stoop to a fax
Every now and again.

Which reminds me, dear Cuz,
Of the fun on the phone.
Not whistles and beeps
Just the regular tone,
With your voice not a screen;
Giving word of your news -
What goes on in the street;
Your political views.

So give us a call
When you're feeling in sync.
I'll drop everything,
Pick it up in a wink.
Then tell us your news
Don't resort to the Net.
The sound of your voice
Is a much better bet.

Bowel-de-Dash

Old Boy, they tell me through the vine,
Or is it "on the street" that news is heard?
That the blood is red and bright
That taints your regal turd!

Good news indeed, for I for one
Know well the official warning.
So welcome now to the All Bran Clan
- a plateful every morning!

Fear not this change in manly diet,
For better far to have the trots
Than a turgid, sluggish tum
That on the inside slowly rots!

Over the Hill?

When you're past the mark of seventy
Its no more a world of plenty;
In fact your life's diminishing -
Quite soon it could be finishing.

So don't expand your world with dreams,
With ideas beyond your means;
Rather start to clean that cupboard -
Its now you who are Miss Hubbard!

Make sure your will is legal still,
Decide who's in charge when you are ill,
Who plans the last ceremony,
Knows which and where the cemetery.

Do you know where is your grave
And who'll your precious china save?
Make sure your books will still be read
In years long after you are dead?

If you and yours are well prepared
Much future anguish may be spared.

Please Check This Baggage Through
A Backward Glance

Please check this baggage through
I won't need it on this flight;
Just check this baggage through
And keep it out of sight.

There's a thing they called a tuck-box
With metal sides and top
It's full of mother's letters
Which I dared not make her stop.
I wrote her back on Sundays
Told her everything was fine
No mention of the beatings
Or how we "toed the line";
The standing in the corner
With hands above the head
The waiting for a caning
With arms and legs of lead;
The fumblings in the bedrooms;
The stabs of guilt and fright;
"Just button up you lip, son,
And keep your mouth shut tight."

   Please check this baggage through
   I won't need it on this flight;
   Just check this baggage through
    And keep it out of sight.

There's a greenish looking duffle
With numbers stamped in black
Some blood and mud and spattered stains
And relics I brought back.
An evil looking smoke-case,
"Widow maker" etched in white
And Christmas propaganda,
Some leaflets dropped at night.
"Go home you Yankee soldier,
You have no business here.
Let us choose between the north
And the south in our Korea".

Tell that to the Sergeant
Whose face was blown to bits
Tell that to the Major
Who died legless at the hips.

Please check this baggage through
I won't need it on this flight;
Just check this baggage through
And keep it out of sight.

There's a multi-coloured hold-all
With labels by the score
Of pubs and camps, and teams and champs
And memories galore;
Of promises that were broken,
Of trysts and trusts, and campus larks.
We studied and we played hard
We made our passing marks.
They said their valediction,
Exhortations and much more;
They gave us benediction
Said the world was at our door.
But the world was not awaiting
Our graduating year
Didn't share our enthusiasm
And our hopes soon turned to fear.

Please check this baggage through
I won't need it on this flight;
Just check this baggage through
And keep it out of sight.

There's a plastic bag of garbage
Some flotsam from the shore
Inhalers and syringes
We had hidden from the law.
We had built our tented cities
In the hope of better days.
In the innocence of youth
We tried to change man's ways.
We faced loggers with our fists;
We stuck spikes in ancient trees;
We slept among the dead heads
That were washed up by the seas.
Against chemicals and dams
We chanted and protested;
We sat-in and were sat upon
Were harassed and arrested.

   Please check this baggage through
   I won't need it on this flight;
   Just check this baggage through
   And keep it out of sight.

Here's a decent looking suit-case,
I might take this one with me;
"Frequent Flyer" writ in gold
For everyone to see.
I left those things behind me

And cut and shaved my hair.
I wear a suit on weekdays
And no-one stops to stare.
We're called the generation
Of hippies that were lost.

But we did not fight in vain
It was worth more than it did cost.
There are whales, there are dolphins

Some rivers and some lakes.
We did just what we had to
We took the risks it takes.

Don't check that suitcase through,
I might need it with me now.
There's memories of who
And why and what and how.

If we didn't stop the clear cut
Our message filtered through;
"You don't lord it over nature,
Have your cake and eat it too."
We're now in from the fringes
We're mainstream and here to stay;
If we didn't win the war
At least we won the day.

Please check the rest right through
I won't need it on this flight.
Just check that baggage through
And keep it out of sight.

Part III – For the Outhouse on the Bay

The Effect It Has

If you don't give a damn
For the state of the land
Or the price of a coke
Or the latest joke

If you don't know the day
Or if its June or May
If you couldn't care less
If the house is a mess

Then it's safe to say
You're in Go Home Bay
For at least a week ...

Insect Wisdom

"You can't take it with you,"
Said the spider to the fly
"I know", said the squito,
"That's why I suck them dry."

But the spider was the wiser
Because he wrapped up his dead
In little silken shrouds
'Till he was ready to be fed.

"So there, little 'squito ..."

The Recipe

To smooth hard rocks
Add a brisk west wind;
Lightly touch with spray;
Garnish with pine trees.
Now close both your eyes
Expose whole to the sun
Relax all your fingers
…and don't pass it on!

On Hearing A Sneeze From The North

I sometimes wonder
When a noise like thunder
Comes wafting on the Georgian breeze
If the Lawson's father
Said, "Sons I'd rather
You vented a roar than a wheeze"!

Part IV – Celebratory

Christmas 1979
(With apologies to Stanley Holloway)

'Twas on the night of Christmas
When Jessica and Dunc,
And Emily and Rupert
And their parents got drunk.

They ate too much, they yelled a lot,
They made a dreadful noise.
The girls they got all giggly
And blamed it on the boys.

And when they got all tired of it
Were ready for some sleep
They began to think a little bit
Of presents they would keep.

They knew in all the noise and fun
A lucky group were they
To have such happy friends around
On such a happy day.

Not everyone they knew
Had had so many toys
Or all the tasty food and fun
That make for Christmas joys.

And when they went to bed that night
They said some thoughtful prayers
And thanked the little Jesus
For the fortune that was theirs.

Marie-Claire
(Mathieu's New Sister)

We went to the hospital
To see what was there
Guess what we found?
We found Marie-Claire.

What was she like?
She had lots of nice hair
Two beautiful eyes
And a long, lovely stare.

Mathieu is Two

Happy Birthday, Mathieu Rupert
Now you've reached the age of two.
You've many words in French, I know,
And in English quite a few.

Happy Birthday Mathieu Rupert
We are glad that we are here
To share your second birthday
With you and Marie-Claire.

Grow up strong and gentle, Mathieu,
Loyal to dad and mother
And share your toys and pleasure
As McClaire's big loving brother.

Mathieu, Bonne Anniversaire,
Une longue et heureuse vie
Soit gentile à Marie-Claire
À son pere et Emily.

Vivi At Four

I know it isn't easy
Being called a name like Vivi
But it helps you get along
When you're beautiful and strong.

And you have an older brother
And a very loving Mother
And a sister named McLaire
And a Dad who's always there.

A Gran Gran who knits you socks
A Gra Pa who has no locks.
And it helps you get along
When you're beautiful and strong.

And then another birthday
Comes roaring right along
And its time to light those candles
And sing that happy song.

Happy Birthday Vivi Henry
Now you've reached the age of four
Oh, its Happy Birthday Vivi
And many birthdays more.

Mathieu at Eight - Haughty and Nautical

I'm a nautical naughty
High, mighty and haughty.
When I'm on the high seas
My head swells like the breeze.

With the wind, I can run;
I can jibe, having fun.
If you think I'm quite daft
Just watch from the aft
When my sails I let breach
At the head of a reach.
If you have any doubt
Watch me come right about
Then you'll know I'm the master
Of my own single-master.

Mathieu's Eighth Birthday

Hurrah, hurrah, today's the day
That Mathieu reaches eight
A day when we all come to say
Whoopee, let's celebrate!

He's only eight but look at what
He's done in that short spell.
On country skis he's really hot
He truly does quite well
Gives just cause for 'Pa to yell
And urge him on in swimming;
Or paddling or rowing yet -
Ribbons he just keeps winning!
But lest his head too swollen get
May he keep his humble charm.
Help others in their quest to win
Keep his sisters free from harm;
Be a teacher and a guide
Showing others how to swim
Or row or sail or ride

A goat, a horse or bat.
But on those days when calm creeps in
Let's turn to quieter pleasures
Like carpentry or paper planes
Or puzzles 'mongst his treasures.
And then perhaps he'll feel the urge
To write a line or two
In diary or scrap book
In future years to view.

But for the moment now
For Mathieu's special day
All join me please and say
Hoorah, Hoorah, Hoorah.

Now raise your glass
And give a clink
For Mathieu's happy day
For Mathieu is a wonderous lad
"May he stay right in the Pink!"

To Mathieu on his Ninth Birthday

Mathieu's nine years old today,
A growing, intelligent boy;
He's fun and likes to joke and play,
His brain he does employ.

He reads a lot and Lego builds,
Makes gifts and useful things with wood.
He uses all his many skills
And mostly does the things he should.

There are the times, I've heard it said,
He'll tease his sisters two;
And when they're 'sposed to be in bed
It is a naughty thing to do.

But all in all he's pretty fine,
In fact he's really great;
And since today he's turning nine
Let's join to celebrate.

Mathieu Turns Eleven

Good Gracious! Good Heaven!
Mathieu's turning eleven.

In just a few years
He's become a strong boy
No more crayons and tears
Seeking challenge not toys.

He can drive his own boat
And paddle a canoe
Sail, swim, dive and float …
Most things he can do.

So wish this young man
More success in his teens
Let him strive as he can
Let him do what he means.

Good luck and fair weather
From Gran Gran and Gra Pa
Always think of the other
Those less lucky by far.

Keep your eyes sharp and keen,
Keep your mind on the course;
On others don't lean;
Be your own driving force.

Ghislain's Fortieth

We don't know at all
If it's a ketch or a yawl
But when Ghislain sets his sail
All competitors pale
At the frightening sight
Of his prowess and might.

So here's a donation
A sail rigged celebration
A sign of our awe
Of our great son-in-law!

A Nautical Forty

The years are most naughty
  Ghislain's turning Forty
And he looks about twenty-nine.

To keep his boats steady
  His line's always ready
Here's a gift of 'fore and 'aft line.

May he keep his looks youthful
  And his muscles most useful
As he passes the forty-year mark.

May he continue to be
  A great Daddy to three
And to Emily a lover with spark.

Ghislain at Forty-Three

Though he's reached the age of forty-three
  His busy life he runs full speed
Each challenge meets with utter glee
  While taking care of every need.

Not content with tiring teaching
  Or river's daily challenges
On bike he's bent on records reaching
  As he tours the Georgian fringes.

Then to Quebec in faith he dashes,
  Family all bundled in the car
Lays to rest his mother's ashes
  With old friends from near and far.

And now he's back to start a term,
  The year before sabbatical,
As passports, plans and mini-vans
  Need energy fanatical.

We wish you all the very best
  In your year of forty-four;
Try to get some well earned rest
  Keep energy in store.

May Parry Sound with joy abound;
  Your house be filled with laughter.
May all enjoy the scenic Fall
  And chill winter's thrills thereafter.

Ode to Kittie-Marie

Kittie-Marie has a birthday today
    And all the world's anxious to hear
Which of life's milestones she's passed
    And which in the future is near.

But she's reached the age of discretion,
    Where silence is better than chatter;
Gentle hint, and lessons well learned
    And kindness, are more to the matter.

Our hope as she goes on life's journey
    Is that we'll continue to be
A part of the health and bright charm
    That we know as our Kittie-Marie.

To John Harris McPhedran
(on presenting a chisel as a birthday present)

To chisel home some finer point
If not to hit the nail upon the head.
But then of course some other use
May suggest itself instead!

To the Somewhat/Sometime Retiring Judge
Douglas Wilkins at 70

The days of rising 'ere daybreak
    To paddle the shores of the bay
To arrive in the city so early
    To serve justice at Queen Street and Bay.

Or cycling with helmet on head
    To the courts of order and law;
Changing jeans for the robes of the office …
    Are not needed, we're told, any more.

Nor needs dear Barbara to languish
    Alone on their wind whipping isle
Tending plants from places exotic;
    Being brave and fronting a smile.

No doubt there's still earth to be carried
    By Doug, and sons Jimmy and Hugh.
To make up for the lack of nutrition
    On the rocks with nutrients few.

But those now gathered around him
    Most surely Doug's future do ponder;
What will he do with his time?
    Will he gaze even further and yonder?

They're known for exotic long journeys
    To countries flung wide and afar
From Darwin's Galapagos Islands
    To Baffin, Bhutan, Panama.

From trails in the hills of Nepal
    To the floes of the Arctic's dark ice
And trips to Antarctica's shore line.
    Say "Travel"; they'll be gone in a trice!

Now Doug got started quite early,
    As with Warren the globe he did trot …

On foot, though neither was burly….
    At least they didn't get shot.

Doug's also well known as a lister
    Of birds, both exotic and rare;
Erratic, eruptive, occasional,
    With his glasses he'll surely be there.

But the question we all have to face
    And Doug no less than the rest …
Is it better to rest on your laurels
    Or keep putting yourself to the test?

They say that for judge's retiring
    There's a role in settling "dispute";
"Conflict resolution" they call it
    It's gaining in clout and repute.

Or will you look down on your court
    Once more strike firm with your gavel,
Turn your back on courts' and precedents,
    Choose the route of ever more travel?

Just enjoy your new found dilemma
    As you pass through the portals of seventy;
With genes like those of your family
    Here's to health and years more a plenty!

So here's to our judge NOT retiring
    But surfing for change mid career!
As they embark on ever more journeys,
    We wish Douglas and Barbara good cheer!

Robin on his Seventieth

They tell me Robin Fraser
    You've reached the age of reason;
The bard's three score and ten,
    Life's more mellow season.

They said its rapid down-hill
    When you pass through sixty's gate;
You've proved the prophets wrong …
    It's just a different state.

Now put the brakes on further
    And take a well earned rest.
Join those artful dodgers,
    Who know they've passed the test.

Let others beat their brains out
    To prove they are the best.
While we smile, condescending,
    And yawn, and stretch, and rest!

Happy Birthday Charlotte

Charlotte has a birthday
    We're not guessing at her age.
Its beyond the stage of giggles
    Say mature, serene and sage.

We're happy in the knowledge
    That her family of three
Are ensconced in Nanton Avenue
    With a Diva roaming free.

Our wishes for dear Charlotte
　　And Charlie, Sheena too
That this is a beginning
　　Of an era bright and new.

Less visits to the hospital
　　Fewer trips away from home
More time alone, to be yourselves
　　Build each their pleasure dome.*

No need to search for Xanadu*
　　Or places far away;
What's wrong with Prairie Winnipeg
　　Or a sea-washed Breton Bay?

So here's to another year
　　A happier, healthier one
With time to be at ease again;
　　Relax, stay home, have fun!

　　*Coleridge's Kubla Kahn

To William Nichols on his Seventieth

When William has a birthday
　　One needs must celebrate
Especially when the milestone
　　Is Septuagenary's gate!
It's three score years and ten they say
　　As the news is cast abroad
Let the Nicholodeons sound
　　To draw the admiring horde!
Some may not bet a "Nichol"

Or even yet a dime
But I'll bet my bottom dollar
   They'll have a marvellous time.

Alas, the Fells have duties
   For birthdays of their own
George's and an in-law
   If the truth be only known.

Now Kittie's brother's sixty
   And George adds one more notch
As William enters seventy …
   It's worth a triple scotch!

So we'll have to toast you, Nichols,
   From places far away
But our thoughts are surely with you
   On this celebratory day.

You're an officer, a gentleman;
   Have served as A.D.C.;
You're a poet, you're a sailor
   And have sailed the great high sea.

They say you're quite a builder
   In town and rural seat;
You're father and a husband
   And as each none can compete.

We're thinking of you, William,
   On this special summer's day.
May the sun keep shining on you
   As we toast you from the Bay.
Here's a toast for Kittie's brother

And one for Georgie Boy!
And the biggest of them all
   For William! – Cheers and Ships Ahoy!

*Written on July 11, (George's birthday), for
William's on July 13*

Kittie-Marie's Birthday
November 24, 2002

I love you for your truant hair
Which needs so much attention;

I love you for your views on life
Which sometimes cause us tension;

I love you for your love of cats
Though cause they are of troubles;

I love you for your honesty
And pricking other's bubbles;

I love you for your strong held views
Even those I think are wrong;

In fact I love you through and through
From morning through the night;

I love you being just yourself
For me you're just all-right!

Uncle Bill at Eighty

It was a day in late October
    In a city called the Soo
At the turning of the century
    When arrived our "You Know Who".

Today we are to celebrate
    And give him three big cheers,
And wish both Peg and William
    Many more such happy years.

Seen through the eyes of Kittie
    Whom they took unto their hearth,
All thoughts of lake and city
    Are of happiness and mirth.

That day she beat our hero
    In Canasta played to win
And those crazy Sunday outings,
    When he took them for a spin.

"Watch it", he'd shout with terror,
    As they cornered on two wheels,
And the family clung together
    With their stomachs in their heels.

And those endless games of snooker,
    Argentinean was his style,
As we made our fruitless efforts
    And he watched us with a smile.
    Those many happy parties
    When they gather all the clan;
And see if George remembers
    Names and faces, if he can.

And those days in bright mid-summer
　　When Bill looks northward to the lake,
And Aunt Peggy with her trowel
　　Would to the garden rather take.

When you think of all their visits
　　It makes your mind go heady,
With Bill a'standing at the door
　　And Peggy "not quite ready".

"Just think" she said "my dear,
　　What confusion we would bring,
If we arrived right on the button.
　　I wouldn't think of such a thing"!

So today we wish Bill happiness
　　As we celebrate four score
And wish our Aunt and Uncle
　　Very many happy more.

Charlie's Eightieth

Now Charlie you know is a hunter
　　Who hails from the rugged mid-west
But it's as an inveterate punster
　　That those gathered here know him best.

You may know his name as a birder
　　His fame as a Brodie Club lister
But you really know nothing of Charlie

　　If you've not heard a Charlie tongue twister.
From "the Leith Police dismisseth us"

To the crowd "sitting, sipping Schlitz"
   And thence to "here I sit and shiver"
      While we "just shivers and sits"!

And don't forget Charlie the drinker
      With a malt that's single or double …
Slang Slainte Bhath to a god who is pagan
      -- A glass in his hand means trouble.

Then there's that side of dear Charlie
      With eyes all sparkle and twinkle;
In stature not small, with tales that are tall
      From naught some humour he'll winkle.

I first met Charlie in Rosedale
      When he stole dear Charlotte away
And returned to the house called Devonshire
      Where Charlotte stood proud on display.

First Rathnally's Republic then Farnham,
      Then Elm were graced with their verve.
Sheena grew from gurgle to giggle
      While Charlotte delish' dinners did serve.

Let's not lose sight of the challenge
      This three-some faced over the years,
All born with stoic good humour
      As they overcame illness and fears.

Then they moved to a Cove called Jersey
      To a farm on a wide windy Bay;
Spent winters in Acady's Wolfville
      Less ice, and it's certain no spray!

And we're glad they haven't deserted
    Their friends who stayed in Mid-East
And grace us with regular visits
    When we share some drinks and a feast!

So please join me now in a toast
    To Charlie who's reached his four score
Here's to Charlie in well malted barley
    "May he thrive many happy years more"!

Nancy at 75 +1

Now Nancy's reached something
In the race we all run
And as Nancy is Nancy
She's reached it plus one.

You see in our Nancy
A committed achiever;
Take reading or swimming
She's a total believer.

There's so many aspects,
Debating or walking
Or "Life's Long(est) Learning"
Or simply just talking.

It's a matter of attitude
It could be just fun;
But better by far
If it's even, plus one!

Where others might dabble
Or play round the edges
Nancy dives for the centre
Parts the weeds and the sedges.

And with her achievements
As she climbs up life's hill,
May she keep her good humour
Her determined good will.

We're all here to wish her
Many more cheerful years;
Just keep those eyes sparkling
Brush away nagging fears.

Happy Birthday, dear Nancy;
With your Aubrey have fun;
Avoid lurking shadows
Keep your face to the sun.
Happy Birthday!

To Ken Ross on his Eightieth?

One day upon the subway
    I wore the old school tie;
I'll never know the reason
    The wherefore or the why.

But on the trip back homeward,
    The year was fifty-seven,
A voice with English accent said
    "You must be sent from heaven."

I blinked and said I knew not
    What was it on his mind.
"You're a Teddy Boy," he said
    "Most fortuitous a find!"

So off we got at Rosedale
    Addresses did exchange
"Here's one be sure to contact,
    Don't lose this precious name."

Now this fellow was not Kenneth
    But he knew the Teddy's crowd
The school we'd all been sent to -
    And his voice was rather loud.

In time I met young Kenneth
    And his family did greet.
And with his growing household
    Did often go to eat.

Some two or more years after
    At a party in their house
I met a girl called Kittie
    Who'd soon become my spouse.

Those days our lives were busy
    But in contact we did keep
As young families we raised
    With little chance to sleep.

Ken came to see a farm
    That we were soon to buy
He stroked his chin in horror
    And said "Oh my, my, my!"

But we couldn't hold a candle
    To Ken's exploits wondrous
His lone sail across the Atlantic
    In gigantic waves and thunderous.

Or his taking up piano,
    Learning music how to read;
Or trading stocks upon the net,
    Hungry hounds at foot to feed.

Nothing's too much trouble
    No hurdle is too high
For a boy who's trained at Teddy's
    - Now you know the reason why.

So join me now, I ask you,
    In a toast to sailor Ken
May he still make tacks and jibes
    As he did in days back then.
(Tacks and Jibes to Ken!)

Fiftieth Anniversary for Peg and Bill

It takes a lot of stamina
    And more of give and take
To work and live through fifty years
    With family and mate.

Times when decisions must be made
    Every day as well as night
When one has reason to turn left
    And the other chooses right.

When Billy's heart to the north is called
    Peg's eyes turn to the flowers
When Bill's all dressed, ready for a date
    Peg needs a few more hours.

Mind you, you wouldn't want to see,
    A mirror image in your spouse.
A Dad who didn't yell or shout
    Or a Mother like a mouse.

Life, you see, is a tug of war
    'Tween spirits not the same
And sweet the marriage à la Peg and Bill,
    Where they both enjoy the game.

We raise our glass and lift our hearts,
    And wish them happy days
And hope the way they live their lives
    Will guide us in our ways.

Beechwood House
(Aunt Marjorie's Last Abode)

Come to friendly Beechwood
    Number 2 on Westbrough Road
Where six retiree ladies
    Have set up joint abode.

Pam, Cathy, Jo and Vera
    Now keep the place together
And help these cheerful women
    Through fine and stormy weather.

The food at lunch and supper
  (Called dinner and high tea)
Is enough to sink a battleship
  For the likes of you and me.

There's potatoes and four veggies
  At every midday dinner.
No wonder they're all eating
  And no one's getting thinner.

Hilda taught those dance routines
  Pamela does the same
Maude's salvation was the army
  Marjorie's the nursing game.

Bessie beats the records
  For great grandchildren, don't you know
While Vi the iron monster
  Finds eating rather slow.

With eyes upon the sky
  Is ever watchful Mabel
While Marjorie, ex matron,
  Does rule the roost at table.

And hovering over all
  Are staff that are terrific,
Who attend to every need
  Both general and specific.

These things you'll soon find out
  If you get a chance to see.
For care and cosy comfort
  Number 2's the place to be.

To John Lawson
"Still Scoring at Four-Score"

A Lawson's a Lawson
   As all of us know;
When they take on a challenge
   It's "Go Lawson, Go!"

Take our hero today
   Our famed Uncle John.
On many a broad front
   He saw, came and won.

The opera for instance,
   Or Roy Thompson Hall,
Making sure opportunities
   Were open to all.

Take the Mendelsson Choir
   And the old Massey Hall
The Faculty of Music
   He supported them all.

Honourary Doctor of Law
   From his old U of T
I could name many more,
   Not just two or three.

The Glenn Gould Foundation,
   Delta Kappa Epsilon,
The Ontario Arts Council;
   Those honours just pile on.

In the Annex at Elgin
   Famed parties John gives
Where overseas students
   Share the house where he lives.

And up at the cottage
   He leads a full life;
Though free to relax,
   Wash away city strife.

Take the wind on the Bay -
   When others are rock-bound
He'll unfurl his new sail
   And head out for the Sound.

Or on swims round his rock
   He surprises us all
As he waves from the water,
   Or gives us a call.

And trips to the Arctic
   Are part of his menu;
If exciting or far flung
   Its John's kind of venue.

Take Southern or Northern
   Or Eastern or West,
Nahanni or Norway
   He'll face challenge with zest.

To be invited to dinner
   Is the joy of his neighbours;
Chicken, beans, apple pie
   Are the fruit of his labours.

Just keep up your efforts,
    Keep showing us how
To live to the full,
    While we smile and say "Wow!"

Happy Birthday, dear John,
    May you have many more.
Best wishes from the Fells
    From your south's rocky shore.

Uncle Arthur on his Eighty-Sixth Birthday

My God, today you're eighty-six!
    What's your secret Uncle Art?
Is it still the drinks you mix?
    Or Janet from that Southern part?

When you return with spring perhaps
    You'll share your secret potion.
Or will you keep it under wraps
    To avert a family commotion!

We wish you well, dear Uncle Art,
    And Janet and friends beside you.
Keep health in body, mind and heart;
    To eighty-seven may Zephyr guide you!

Uncle Stewart on his Ninetieth

We've come to honour Stewart
    Our nonagarian new;
We've come as sons and daughters
    Nieces and nephews too.

From Sarnia and Binghampton
　　From places east and west;
We've come with one accord
　　To wish him all the best.

He comes from lineage Waspish
　　As you all here should know.
His noble looks and forceful jaw
　　His clear resolve do show.

He's a model to us all,
　　With stretches and cold shower;
And visits to the tuck shop
　　At the appointed hour.

His rituals are habitual;
　　His stogie fills the air -
Then he opens up the window
　　Draws oxygen out there!

He learned typing from his sister;
　　At U of T debated;
Was on the rowing team;
　　With honours graduated.

He's serious but he's funny;
　　"Now tell me George", he says;
"What make you of the economy
　　In these globalizing days?"

But "By Golly!" and "By Gosh!"
　　He puts us all to shame;
He remembers all our foibles;

Forgets no face or name.

So you just keep on going,
   Stick with that health regime,
And keep these birthdays coming
   Dear R.E. Stewart Green.

Uncle Stewart at Ninety-Four

Now Uncle Stewart fooled them all;
If he's not standing tall
At ninety-four still holding court -
What's to sell, what be bought!
The New Yorker still he reads right through
And tells you then what you should do;
From its pages dense, wisdom does dispense
To those with patience and the sense
To listen; thus we rally to his name
As he now spreads his sprawling frame,
With "Well Now!", "By Golly" and "By Gad"
We listen to our trusted Dad,
Or Poppy, Uncle, Cousin, Friend.
Or just the man with whom to spend
Some time to relish from the past
Some lessons learned, so they may last.

Bass Passes the Buoy of 70

When Mariner Commander Bass
   Enters the port of seventy,
It bodes well to polish the brass,
   Bring gifts, best wishes a'plenty.

So Kittie and George here wish you,
        Their chum, asthmatic and wheezing,
Many happy returns, and much tissue,
        And strength to withstand all the teasing.

May your sails continue to billow
        With Juliette your last and First Mate;
May you dream sweet dreams on your pillow
        - Not rise in the morning too late.

So now to his very best friend
        Old Forky is happy to give
A print by his very own hand
        And long, happy years may he live.

To Victoria on her Wedding
to Gerrard Daniel Evans

We'll yell a Fells Whoop
From the top of the poop;
Bid the Gulf Stream's warm breeze
Waft across the broad seas
Our wishes of joy and fulfilment.
May your days spent together
Be filled with much pleasure
With the strength to be tough
When the going gets rough;
With time for reflection
And warmth and affection;
A life that has space for contentment.

Helen and Duncan

When Helen from the mountains
    Met young Duncan of the Fells
There were tremors on Vesuvius
    And the sound of wedding bells.

A Fell you know is high land
    So it was no accident
That Helen was attracted
    To this tall and handsome gent.

Yes, it was by providence
    That our Duncan grew up tall
Musical and athletic;
    He could throw a mighty ball.

In summer month's regattas
    He'd win a string of medals
In spring and fall he shifted
    Gears, to pushing bikes and pedals.

In winter he put on skis
    And went through all his paces;
But his skills upon the hills
    Didn't win him any races.

Then Helen did the Australian thing
    Went travelling for a year
And Duncan took a six months fling
    To try the western beer.

No slouch herself, our bridal queen
    Combines with charming looks

A determination quite supreme
   With skills of keeping books.

Yes, she is good at figures
   He at throwing darts;
He has many muscles;
   She has lots of smarts.

No wonder then the two did meet
   Being lonely far from home
When Helen in the "Y" did great
   This lone and handsome drone.

And love did raise its wondrous head
   And spun them on their heels;
Then not an hour was spent apart
   Including nights and meals.

Then Helen for her home did part
   Leaving Duncan full of sighs;
Until Duncan set his mind and heart
   To cross the Orient skies.

Now Helen then worked miracles,
   Seeing good potential;
Releasing Duncan's manacles
   From things inconsequential.

Now we hope this combination
   Of their talents intertwined
Will reward their determination
   With a future that's sublime.

To Liz and Rupert

There's nothing like a boy's school
   For meeting future brides;
That's what they say of Rupert
   Who's surfed the world's wide tides.

He's surfed with much excitement
   On the Gorge's evil reaches;
He's ridden bucking currents
   Carve-jibed off Maui's beaches.

He found time to go to Western;
   In geography graduated;
By day he pulled an oar,
   Most nights he marinated!

Armed with studies done in business
   He counted coins for the Mint.
But the company lost the contract
   Gave Rupe the "exit" hint!

But chalk it up to knowledge
   On life's long learning curve;
Like publishing in London …
   Rupe does it all with verve.

Meantime where's our Elizabeth
   Whom Rupe met in his teens?
Well, she's just doing nicely
   No slouch by any means.

Off to U. New Brunswick
    For a degree in sports and fitness;
Be careful not to cross her
    Or her strength you'll surely witness!

So Rupert has it all now
    Fitness and yoga too
And Liz ain't doing badly
    'Cause its "coffee time" for two!

So let's toast this Ridley couple.
    May their dinghies not be leaky;
May their parents treat them fondly
    And their children not be cheeky!

To Adrienne and Graham

There's something quite catching
About the Ketcheson clan
A fact that dear Adrienne
Can now understand!
Look at Graham's parents;
At Don with his plans
And Phyllis her pottery
And her watering cans;
And properties wide flung
Like the Lake of the Woods
And the house in Pradines …
Wow! Some chattels, some goods!
Now Graham's no loafer
And Adrienne's no slouch
They've bought their own place
With a room for the couch,
With acreage thrown in;
Three bedrooms to boot
And all this convenience
Close by Parry Sound (Hoot).
Where Adrienne writes newsletters
Graham tripping quite bold,
Canoes in the summer
And skis in the cold;
And then there's the drums
Which in their country retreat
Our Graham can practice -
Set the woodlands abeat.
It sounds like the coupling
Of a well suited pair,
And we are all happy

Their nuptials to share.
Health and much happiness
To our newly wed pair,
A life of fulfilment,
Many pleasures to share,
Whether on the Nahanni
Or skiing down hills;
Whether cresting life's waves
Or suffering through spills.
Raise your glasses on high
And join us again!
"A life of much pleasure
With minimum pain."

Determined David

He's not called determined for nothing,
Our groom from the farmlands of Mono.
Though it's hard to know what he's thinking,
For him just nothing's a No-No.

From the old school-house on the side-road
And Elsie Anderson's care,
He mounted the bus to the big school
And the challenge that awaited him there.

Not one to report to his parents
The ups and downs of the day,
His marks went from average to better,
As David made steady headway.

But despite the rigours of school work.
The calm of the hillsides was rent

With the roar of mini and trail-bike,
With David and Stephen hell-bent.

Then his fancy for two-wheels subsided
And his serious side soon prevailed;
With marks not at all unimpressive,
For Ryerson he determinedly sailed.

To Toronto he shyly was guided
To the Fells who afforded protection.
Paul Erwin came to his rescue,
Then completed young David's defection.

Not content with his Ryerson diploma,
Our David set goals more severe
And embarked on a series of courses
To further his budding career.

Now it may've been hard on his mother
When the table was covered with books,
And a computer spilled out its data
In an area more suited to cooks.

But months of deep concentration
And days of study, no cheer,
Gave rise to a full fledged degree
And the title of Prof. Engineer.

Meanwhile the cars in the driveway
Had changed from Pan Am to Corvette;
With a stint in a Volkswagon Rabbit,
Now matured to antique Chevrolet.

But, Hark! the sounds of construction
And a house rising up on the hill
Gave rise to some new speculation.
Was our Jack looking out for his Jill?

Oh, Joy, he then met dear Mary.
We knew it was a matter of time
Till David would work his deft magic
And make Mary bring toe to the line.

He's not called determined for nothing,
You can see from the story we tell.
Now let's toast the newly wed couple
May they live long, happy and well.

Sheena's Wedding Toast

Nothing can be meaner
Than a slightly angry Sheena
Whose been thwarted from the way she wants to go.

Nothing can be keener
Than a quite determined Sheena
Who's decided on the way she wants to go.

Try never to demean her
Or our ever watchful Sheena
Will one up you before you really know.

Now never get between her
And the goals of forceful Sheena
Or she'll tell you clear as daylight where to go.

When Teener was a teaser
There was none could hold our Sheena
From digging out the truth she chose to know

If you have never seen her
As a sailing skipper Sheena
Then you've never seen a laser really go.

There's nothing shines as sheener
Than the glamour side of Sheena
When she's dressed up with a place she wants to go.

Now its time to ween her
From this family of Sheena's
Yes, its time to let our Sheena go

Yes its time for Filowytch
To end this two year itch
And tie the loving knot with cupid's bow.

Now toast this happy couple
With joy and love most supple
As now off in happiness they go.

Nancy and Aubrey/Eb and Jane
28th Wedding Anniversary

On a wintry night in Kingston
In the year of fifty-one
There took place an introduction
And the saga had begun.

Kittie was the catalyst
And kept a yearly score.
It wasn't love at first sight
Five years it took or more.

There were comings and some goings
And some goings-on at Maple.
Then the comings were more frequent
And romance became a staple.

Meanwhile around the corner
On an avenue called Nanton
On a floor above our Kittie
Arrived two damsels wanton.

Then came the year of '57
And Jane was spliced with Eb
And Nancy caught her Aubrey …
Leaving Kittie still a deb.

But all those years of waiting
And those Saturdays of hell
Were worth our Kittie's patience
When she met her plural Fell.

Now many years have passed us
Leaving signs of wear and tear
But we're happy we're together
To enjoy another year.

So we'll raise our glasses higher
To celebrate endurance.
It maybe that we're lazy
Or just need some assurance.

But it sure beats changing partners
And the singles circuit bar.
Perhaps it's that we're happy
Quite happy as we are.

So here's to Eb and Jane
And Aub and Nancy too!
May their anniversaries be many
And their troubles rare and few.

Aubrey and Nancy - 1997
On Forty Years of Marriage

When "Aub" and "Nance" began the dance
   Of marriage in '57
Who was that seen, who shed a tear
   And said "Its made in heaven!"

Like me or you, or any two,
   Who start the trip of marriage
There's giving here and taking there
   As rides the bridal carriage.

But out the gate, at prodigious rate,
   They started having babies
We caste a glance, we looked askance
   And said "Is this real, or maybe?"

So Nancy scrubbed and Nancy rubbed
   While Aubrey's clientele developed.
The kids grew tall, the house grew small
   As domestic life enveloped.

Then figure they their needs are bigger
    So to Russell's Hill repaired them.
With many beds for exhausted heads
    … the taxman never spared them.

With ups and downs and sometimes frowns
    Russells spread their wings about them
Came days of sadness, days of gladness
    As progeny lived without them.

Then came those days when Aubrey says
    "We need less space to handle."
They clipped their wings, sold off some things
    … No babies now to handle!

Throughout this tale, o'er hill and dale,
    Their Palgrave farm presided;
For one and all, in Spring and Fall
    A home from home provided.

Now we are here, to applaud and cheer
    This achievement matrimonial.
With happy clink, we rise and drink
    In joyous ceremonial.

Christmas 1980

And now again its Christmas
    The time for more good cheer
And the Fells and other friends
    Welcome Bill and Peggy here.

It's great to have a family
　　When one's own is wearing slim
And to know that Bill and Peggy
　　Will be there through thick and thin.

And we welcome all our cousins
　　And our friends from overseas
And Rupert and young Jessica
　　And cats and dogs, with fleas.

Its great to have a party
　　With all ages at the table
When there's cheer for simply everyone
　　Both young and not so able.

When all are getting tired
　　And the children are quite peeved,
We should say a thank you prayer
　　For the nice things we've received.

And also lets remember
　　To thank our Kittie dear
For all her work and patience
　　In providing such good cheer.

To Julian & Juliette

I woke-up on the mid-night,
Rhymes ringing in my ear;
I shook my sleepy head
And searched both far and near
For reasons sympathetic
For this message telepathic.

Then reality came wafting
Across the roiling ocean …
The Bass's celebration
Was causing this commotion.

So on this great occasion
Old Forky and his Kittie
Send many happy wishes
With this celebrating ditty.

To be there was most tempting
But we really couldn't make it.
To have had it otherwise
We'd really have to fake it!

But we look forward to the Fall
And the Teddy's celebrations;
Cruising down the Isis,
Sharing nautical libations.

Meanwhile we send our wishes
For many years of fun together;
May Bass still steer his frigate
Whether fair or foul the weather.

For Julian Alone

And to the ageless brigand of Chichester
Many years may your britches still stir … Sir!

To Geddes & Ruth
(On their 40th Wedding Anniversary)

We are here to celebrate
    An accomplishment now rare …
A splice of man and wife
    For more than forty year!

Ruth was from the West Coast
    And Geddes from the East;
So they settled in the middle …
    A compromise, at least.

Now Hawaii has its sunshine
    And the States a certain pull
But nothing like our Bay Street
    - the caprice of bear and bull.

So between Toronto's skyline
    And the rolling hills of Mono
Our loving, listless couple
    Moves like a swinging yoyo!

If you scan the hills around you
    There's a sight you're sure to see
There'll be Ruth in garden weeding
    As Geddes prunes a tree.

And when the junk of ages
    Became much too much to bare,
They tossed it in the old barn
    And held an auction there.

And then they built a new shed
   For wood and working tool,
Where Geddes keeps his tractor
   And co-management's the rule.

Yes, there've been some downers
   As Geddes rode the tide.
But what's a Windy Craggy,
   When Ruth is by your side.

To pass the winter's long nights
   They take on puzzled jig-saws
While Geddes in the day time
   Makes walking sticks with big saws!

And as for all the children
   They come and go with ease.
Though reactions allergic
   Cause some a stressful sneeze.

And then there's wagging "Ted"
   Who ranges far and wide,
Who goes from sniffing groundhogs
   To an elevator ride.

Of ups and downs together
   This is the merest inkling
But forty years of marriage
   And their eyes are still a-twinkling.

So join me, if you will now,
   And toast our feted pair
Show them that in the future
   Their friends will all be there.

Alvin and Jenny's Tenth Anniversary

Its ten years since that autumn day
    When Jenny and Alvin wed,
And we did for them our blessings pray
    With many a kind word said.

You knew it all was meant to be,
    When they said their wedding vows.
They'd navigate through heavy seas;
    No storm a-smashing their bows.

Now Jen still rides her mower round
    With cheerful smile and looks of pride;
And Alvin does his fence posts pound
    With a confidence that's hard to hide.

Its honesty and much hard work
    A little humour thrown in too,
That parts the clouds that often lurk
    And make you wake up feeling blue.

And so it is with this good pair,
    Who putting problems to the side,
Have built a life that's good and fair
    To help them cope with life's strong tide.

We wish them many years to come;
    Of happiness, joy, good health;
A life that's honest, spiced with fun,
    Where contentment conquers wealth.

To Anne Schlegel

There's an empty room in our house
  The bed all ready and made;
A desk and a dressing table
  And a fireplace freshly laid;

An extra place set for breakfast
  With the fork laid up-side down;
There's some oat-meal porridge waiting
  For Anne in her dressing gown.

There's need for help in the kitchen
  For Kittie to get through the day;
For some French style cookies and crepes
  Made Anne's inimitable way.

Where's the bubble of laughter upstairs?
  The chatter and eager discussing?
The screeching of Mitsubishis?
  Her saying "that's quite disgusting!"

There's no one here in the day-time
  To give Snowy a care-free walk;
There's no one writing a diary
  Or eager to have a good talk.

A violin stands in the corner
  Wondering where Anne can have gone;
And Emily's cello is waiting
  For the joy of a happy sing-song.

Duncan won't rise in the morning;
  George is worried about deals;

116

Kittie has just lost her glasses;
   Emily's at sister Cecile's!

So life on Nanton goes on, Anne
   But we do miss having you here;
So keep in mind, Schlegel Baby,
   Canada and France are quite near.

If ever you feel like travelling,
   Or in need of a change in pace;
There's a family living on Nanton
   Who would welcome your smiling face.

Snowy will howl on the door step
   And Duncan will say "Matsubish!"
Emily will shout "wicked wag!"
   And Kittie will give you a kiss.

Meantime we want you to know, Anne,
   That Em looks forward with pleasure
To time with the Schlegel famille
   To absorb French at her leisure.

Christmas '81

Here's to good old Christmas,
   And lots of Christian cheer;
Here's to old St. Nicholas,
   It's nice to have you here.

Santa Claus came early
   And wakened us with glee,
To come and see what goodies
   He left us by the tree.

You've never seen such chaos
   So early in the day
We opened up the presents
   To look for things to play.

Pat and John gave dinner
   Muff and Marc came too;
Duncan made the hard-sauce
   Emily the cranberry goo.

Kittie brought the salad
   George his new red vest;
Jessica flapped her eye-lids,
   And Rupert looked his best.

It isn't every family
   Or every girl and boy
Who've spent the Christmas season
   In happiness and joy.

We're lucky and we know it.
   As we sing and have a dance,
Let's be mindful of those others,
   Who may never have the chance.

Declining the Invitation (to Scotland)

When we received your invitation,
   It caused a great sensation.
Across the Atlantic ocean
   A positive commotion!

Could we break all bounds of logic
   In efforts psychologic
To participate in person
   Ere our faculties should worsen?

But our plans for Transatlantic
   Excursions most romantic
Had been settled for September
   To fan the dying ember.

To Venice and to Britain
   On that idea we are smitten
So with heavy hesitation
   We decline your invitation.

To Anne and Family

At least it's no longer couplets
   Scanned neatly and ending in rhyme.
Now it's the lines out of carols
   That caress us at Christmas time.

There's little to do in return
   But wish you all much of the best.
For Christmas's festive season
   Have loads of good cheer and much jest!

Ken Haddock

Oh, the tractor's plugged in
And I'm ready to go!
I'll hitch up my plough
And I'll show you how
I'll just scatter that snow
In a moment or three
Just snap your tough fingers
And leave it to me.

Oh, the tractor's plugged in
And I'm ready to go!
I'll get me a cable
And as fast as I'm able
I'll give you a tow
Right out of that lane
Just snap your fingers
And call out my name.

Oh, the tractor's plugged in
And I'm ready to go!
You say there's a car
That's gone in the ditch
Don't give it a thought
I'll give it a hitch
Just call out my name
You're on the road once again.

Oh! the tractor's plugged in
And I'm ready to go!
You said you've got wood
That's not ready to burn
Let me get my keen splitter
And I'll make that dumb critter
Just smile in your grate
Like an sparkling glow worm.

Oh! the tractor's plugged in
And I'm ready to go!
They call me Ken
'cause I'm all in the know
If its a hitch or a pull
Or a plough or a fall
Just call out my name
I've got the answer to all.

Oh, the tractor's plugged in
And I'm ready to go!
Call out my name
And I'll show you just how
With a hitch or a splitter
A dozer or plough.
My God!
Let me show you just how!

In Praise of Bubbly

Nor bear nor bull
Has half the pull
Of a magnum of sparkling bubbly.
Now stocks may rise
Or halve their size
While champers will reward you doubly.

    * * *

While all that glitters is not gold
And stocks may lose their flavour,
Champagne's rewards for those who hold
Is pure pleasure there to savour.

    * * *

Now take a case of champers
And hide it in the vault
So future picnic hampers
Won't suffer by default!

A wise and sure investment
Its rewards are measured doubly
In taste and prestige salient …
Such are the allures of bubbly.

To Cousin Mary

Hi, Cousin Mary
Of Binghamton Town.
We searched for a missive
But none could be found,
Except little short notes
By some marketing grouch
And what fun you were having
On your newly bought couch.

This conversing by E-mail
I find somewhat iffy.
Touch some keys and a mouse
And its off in a jiffy.
I'm stuck in a groove
With my paper and pen
Though I stoop to a fax
Every now and again.

Which reminds me, dear Cous,
Of the fun of the phone.
Not whistles and beeps
Just the regular tone,
With your voice, not a screen,
Giving word of your news -
What goes on on the street;
Your political views.

So give us a call
When you're feeling in sync.
I'll drop everything,
Pick it up in a wink.
So tell us your news
Don't resort to the Net.
The sound of your voice
Is a much better bet.

Liz has been Called to the BAR

We celebrate Liz Tinker.
　No soldier sailor she.
Despite the work and effort
　A lawyer she chose to be.

By dint of perseverance
　And nights in study fraught
She followed in Dad's footsteps
　Mastered cases and the torts.

We will cheer her from the North.
　We will cheer her from afar.
We'll lavish her with presents
　That glorify the Bar.

So here's a Bar of chocolate,
　And some sauce for Bar–b–q,
A bag for Barf, Barcardi,
　And some Bargains, one or two.

There's a Barbie doll included,
　Dressing for salad Bar.
A bagel for the 'mitzvah.
　Is that taking things too far?

But if one day you wake up
　And wonder what you are.
There's a plenitude of choices
　For deciding on which Bar.

Ode to the Frolicking Firemen

On a day in deep mid-summer
   Go Homers heard the call
To attend the Firemen's Frolics
   And answered one and all.

Came Vern Chapman from the Township
   Paul Corrigan in tow
All the way from hot Kenora
   Good methods us to show.

When eventually recovered
   From the crowd upon the rock
Paul gave us words of wisdom,
   Of our crews took steady stock.

It is said in higher quarters
   He really was impressed
Lest we become conceited
   Remember what he stressed …

Take spare gas, spark plugs and a pair of pliers
Nozzles and screwdriver to help you fight the fires.
Boot-up, size-up, avoid any wrinkle
Listen to your Captain and speed up your sprinkle.

Dedicated to the OBDDS, the DOBD's, the Fire-Flites, the Monumentals and all other would be firefighters.

To Bill Graham
New Leader of the Liberal Party

So here's to Bill Graham
    On his well deserved appointment.
Too bad he suffered mayhem
    To achieve this just anointment.

To Barber Bill

My barber Bill
Is quick and deft;
He trims the right
He trims the left.
He clears my ears
Of greying tufts;
What's left on top;
He blows and fluffs.

So thank you, Bill,
For making much
Of my bald pate.
With your deft touch.

Dear Mary
(My long suffering secretary)

How could I live without Mary?
The thought is utterly scary.
Just who would decipher my scrawl
Making sense out of nothing at all?
And who would type all those letters
Free me from key boarding's fetters?

So keep well, dear Mary, please do;
For chaos would reign without you.

To the Chars
Thanks and Celebration

Here's hello from Georgian Bay
   To our friends the Maritime Chars
Who live so very far away
   It might as well be Mars!

George gives you thanks with poetic pen
   For the gift you gave to celebrate
His passing years three score and ten -
   Though sad it is to calibrate.

Now with this present from you two
   To clearly mark the winding way
And fill with fun those eastern routes
   Another trip brooks no delay.

But in the time twixt then and now
   We'll view Char's celebration.
We may be seen as "o'er the hill"
   But the thrill's acceleration!

So have a happy day dear Char
   Look forth to many more.
Your friends from inland waters far
   Are blowing kisses from their shore.

To Maurice,
The Humoristic Carpenter and Helper of All

There was a young man called Maurice
Whose stories matched those of Horace.
They were wise and convoluted
Even sometimes polluted;
But the worst problem of all
Is they were long and would stall
Like an angry sharp-shooter
Our most humble computer,
Causing fear and confusion
Even sometimes delusion
Amongst the old and the frail
For whom the speedy E-mail
Is like a wasting disease.

So Maurice, will you please
Without shedding a tear
Keep it short and quite clear;
Don't tax the old brain
Or it will go down the drain.
But the good news you should know
Is that a "centrex low flow"
In Emily's safe keeping
Is from eyes of Tom's peeping
Hidden, just waiting the call
That you're ready to install.
Em's number you know
- 746, nine, oh, eight, oh!

Christmas 1982

Here's to good old Christmas
    And lots of Yuletide cheer;
Here's to Aunts and Uncles
    And friends from far and near

Here's to Duncan's Birthday
    And presents by the ton;
Here's to Rupe and Jessica
    And whoops of joy and fun.

Here's to Gordon Duncan
    And his pretty daughters three
Here's to absent loved ones
    Who live across the sea.

Here's to Hardy Senior
    And Dorothy and Muff;
Here's to Emily's boyfriend,
    And all that kind of stuff.

And though its very jolly
    And happy for us here
Let's not forget the thousands
    Who are sad this time of year.

Remember those who're jobless,
    Or who've lost a cherished friend;
Or haven't got the money
    On such niceties to spend.

As we raise our glass to Christmas
   And good old Uncle Nick
Let's think of those less fortunate
   Those lonely and those sick.

And while we're on the subject
   Of the forgotten and the least,
Let's not forget our Kittie,
   Who provided all this feast.

So here's to Christmas spirit!
   Let's keep it, you and me,
Not just this day of Christmas
   But through all of '83.

Christmas at the Hardy's

We pray for those unhappy
   Or alone, or sick in bed;
For those who've lost a loved one,
   Or who live in fear and dread.

We hope we will appreciate
   How lucky we have been
And never take for granted
   All the blessings we have seen.

We thank our friends the Hardy's
   Who've been super hosts today.
And now they're round the corner,
   We hope they're here to stay.

To Pat and John C. Hardy,
    To Rupert, Muff and Jess,
The Fells now raise their glasses,
    And wish them all the best.

Spring in Najac

Bring me soon back
To old Najac
Where the Goths
And the Visi Goths came
And Ac
Is the end of a name.

Tell me you know
Where three rivers flow
Through gorges
Carved out of rock;
The Tarne,
Aveyron and the Lot.

Sing me a song
Of Carcasonne
Where La Cité
Rises proudly on show;
The town
Kneeling humbly below.

Lead me astray
In fields of fresh hay
Where the vine
Still clings to the hill;
The air - is gentle and still.

Ode to Pradines

Let me sing you a yarn
Of the Lot and the Tarn
And the falls of Aveyron.

Where on every high rock
There's a castle on top
And a cluster of houses below.

The Romans came first
With unquenchable thirst
To conquer the Gallic will.

Then followed the Goth;
And in spite of God's wrath
The Albigensian heresy.

With crusaders on horse
The English of course
Aided the tale of destruction.

And in spite of it all
There survived the true Gall
Endowed with politeness and charm.

He'll welcome you here
And lend you his ear
As long as you've time for a yarn.

When you look at the walls
Built by Romans and Galls
You see that there's plenty of time.

Lull me to sleep
   On the edge of the deep
Where cocks will crow to the dawn
   And bells will ring in the morn.

By wayside cross
   Remember the loss
Of wars that have ravaged with shame,
   Bruising each family name.

Give me a smile
   I can keep for while
On the face of a farmers wife
   Then I'll know there's hope in this life.

Help me remember
   In the depths of December
The sight of birds on the wing
   The scents that will always be Spring.

I'll soon be back
   To old Najac
Where the Goths and the Visi-Goths came
   And Ac is the end of a name.

The castles will stay
When you've gone on your way
As they did with Goth and the Hun

There's a place called Pradines
That few people have seen
Hugging the edge of a gorge.

If you say you won't dare
This secret to share
You can even stay here for awhile.

So slow down and be calm
And breathe in the charm
The ages have etched in Pradines.

"From W(V)IF to WOF and Bark Again"
*(On the occasion of George Fells' retirement
    from the Board of Working Ventures)*

When a fellow like Jim
Has a visionary whim
You don't take it lightly
In fact you jump sprightly.

In the midst of one night
The idea that was right
Was that the chap in the street
With the rich should compete
To put his hard earnings
Behind entrepreneurs' yearnings.

So Jim hired a guru
To find out just who
And how such a scheme
Might arise from his dream.
He found a young lady,
And I don't mean just maybe,
Saying "Do me a study
With results clear, not muddy!"
Then MacDonald, named Mary,

From mountains to prairie
Did research that proved
(And the government approved -
In fact so impressed
They 15 mill did invest) -
The scheme was worth trying
No kidding, no lying!
So with much fuss and fanfare
And Jim as first Chair
They launched Working Ventures
- Equity, no debentures.

Now despite all the fuss
There wasn't much rush
To take up the offer
Ron Begg was to proffer.

But, by God, then at last
With critics aghast
They raised 400 mill …
And the critics were still!

Their snideness they buried
To register they hurried;
An industry was born
And did Jim blow his horn!

Now WVF
At the gate was not left;
In fact it did well
As its coffers did swell -

Eight hundred mill
Was filling the till.

But the task was quite daunting
And the days of our flaunting
Were fast put to rest
As we tried to invest
At a rate never seen
Up Bay Street to Queen!
From leather to golf course,
To smooth talkers or coarse;
From service to smoke-stack
To manufacturing and back,
To high-tech and I.T.;
… No time for high tea!

Ron and his men
Just showed the world then
How to get cash out fast …
How could the pace last?

Well to tell you the truth
And not be uncouth
They bloody well showed them
The debt that was owed them
For starting a sector
With no guiding vector.

Well, what a surprise!
The value did rise
Touching 18, the summit
… And then did it plummet!

Well, the critics did crow
"We told you just so.
The business of venture
Is no secure debenture
To be spread all around
To every last clown."

So the mighty and high
Had to eat humble pie,
As the balloon from aloft
Made a landing not soft.

And the Board none too soon
Chose a sweeping new broom
To bring in some change
Both in scope and in range.

And under Chair Ian
Though his reign is no paeon
Our feet are well grounded
Though the "NAV" is still pounded.

Then fresh from the West
At the Board's strong request
Came a Vancouver based bevy
Led by David R. Levi.
Les pulled in the reins
Took some losses and gains
Put feet on firm ground
For a long turn-around.

And expectations internal
As well as external
Are clearly now grounded
On reality well founded.

Now the saga I told
Is not new, but quite old;
Is repeated each day
In this world's crazy way.
But the questions remain
…Can our memories retain?
Can we learn from a lesson?
Can our hubris we lessen?
Or are we bound to repeat
A former defeat?

Let's hope its not so!
Let our investments now grow,
And may those who now follow
Not find my words hollow!

The Emancipation of Susie

There's an extra day in Feb this year
    And its there to celebrate
The final split of our Susie dear
    From her worldwide feted mate.

In fact there are reasons all around
    To propose a toast these days;
May she now dance again to music's sound,
    While he with codes of science plays.

We took no side in the past dispute
    And we cast neither blame nor guilt;
Let each enjoy their own repute;
    No tears over life's spilt milk!

Please Behave

When you're able, Mabel,
Please leave the table.
There are others -
Sisters, friends and brothers -
Who are better able,
When at the table,
With manners to behave.
Then all of us can save
A sense of civility,
If not of dignity.
So out the door,
You stupid bore!
Just go to bed
You swollen head!

Red Carpet at the Millers

For whom is the red carpet
Laid out at the door?
Are you waiting for royalty
Or perhaps even more?
Whatever the reason,
Whatever the cause,
It's now quite in season
To greet Santa Claus!

Mary On Your Graduation

Thank you for your invitation
To your splendid graduation.
While we wish we could be present
At your life-time's once event,
You do understand, we are sure,
That we're stuck to this rocky shore,
While you do strut with hood and gown
And we admire from out of town.
Congratulations, cousin Mary!
Your achievements are just scary!

To Our Dear Susie

Now Susie, what stroke is this
That struck you down and makes you miss
The party meant to celebrate
A life of fun, not hibernate
In some aseptic pastelled room
Where joie de vivre gives way to gloom?

So get you out today or soon
Encouraged by the waxing moon.
Enjoy instead a stroke of luck
As sounds from harpsichord they pluck
And you again do dance and play
With those who love you and now miss
Those happy times; a playful kiss
As Susie strokes piano keys
And spirits lift upon a breeze
Of hope and fun, with friends around;
Laughs and songs to a cheerful sound!

We miss you now, our Susie dear,
So come home soon so we can cheer
And once again may dance and sing;
And strokes of bells, not hell, will ring.

Susie on the Mend

Now Susie's on the road to mend,
Curving round most every bend;
In fact, hell bent for leather,
She's cruising in all kinds of weather.
Quite soon she'll be her former self,
A playing pixie, a charming elf.
Go Susie, Go.

Visit of Grandchildren
March 2004

Hey, diddle diddle
The toast's on the griddle
When it's quite done
We will have fun!

Yum! Yum! Yum!

Mrs. Sippi, Marylin
Would not take the garbage in,
But Mrs. Sippi Marilyn,
Couldn't take the garbage in.

How did Mrs. Sippi Marylin
Ever take the garbage in?

Mrs. Sippi Marylin
Had a neighbour who dropped in.
When she saw the garbage bin
She said, "I will take the garbage in!"

Lucky, lucky,
Mrs. Sippi Marilyn

Amy

Here's to Doctor Amy
May her travels far be fair
In New Zealand may she flourish
Have fun in practice there.

When she comes back home again
May she find a fitting slot
For her skills and talents many.
As Canucks we need the lot!

Part V – The Cheer Leader

Be a Sport

If sport is taught
To bring you fame
And make you money,
It's no more a game.

You play for fun
And if you score
A fine home run
You enjoy it more.

But if you lose
Or the game's a tie
Don't blow a fuse
Or ask "Oh, why?"

It's a game you play
To enjoy, have fun.
Let no one say
"If we'd only won."

To lose with grace
To say "well done"
To shake their hands
And share the fun

Is better far
Than hang your head
And shake your fist
Wish you were dead.

So be a sport
And play for fun

Just hope next time
It's your home run.

Stand and be Counted

There used to be a saying
   When I was keen and young
That to give your life to service
   Was good and much more fun

To give your life to others
   To help your fellow man
To "stand up and be counted"
   Never be "an also ran"

It's a motto I now mutter;
   It's tougher by the day,
To voice it without stutter
   As muscles dull and fray.

At Sixty-Five

At sixty-five
I'm still alive
The Transit gives me discounts.

The drugs I need
To keep up speed
Are even getting cheaper.

Now in a bar
Or subway car
They call me Sir or Mister.

So I can take
A pain or ache
The price of being "senior".

It's a better lot
Than a screaming tot
Or an anxious angry teener.

Or a know it-all
Who's standing tall
In the arrogance of thirty.

I've had my thrills
I've climbed those hills
I'm enjoying looking backwards.

I'll take respect
On the quarter deck
Like a crusty ancient mariner.

I'll take salutes
From raw recruits
And toss them words of wisdom.

And when I'm gone
They'll sing this song
With no changes for the better.

When comes the time
They'll say this rhyme
And the truth will not be better.

Ben

Benjamin, Benjamin
Benjamin Barnes
Tell them the truth,
Dispense with the yarns;
Swallow your tact
Just give them cold fact.
It's a lot more fun
If justice is done,
For the truth will out
Without any doubt.

So put on your gown
And head for the court.
Bone up on the facts
Review the right tort;
Tell 'em it straight
And don't hesitate.
For justice delayed
Is justice too late.

So go with it Barnes
Dispense with your charms;
Put on your court livery
Slow down your delivery;
Look the judge in the eye,
And tell him just why,
In voice that's unwaverable
You seek judgement that's favourable.

Saved by the OMB

They came with perseverance;
    They came from every region;
To stop the wretched severance,
    They turned out by the legion.

The battle wasn't local
    There were principles at stake;
They wouldn't be too vocal;
    They avoided that mistake.

They hired a well-known planner
    To make their honest case,
And so with polished manner,
    The "hearing" she did face

We hoped the "hearing" Chair
    Was taken with her pleading'
And the forty people there
    Were worthy of her heeding.

But the wheels of legal process
    They turn in turgid style;
But better slow in progress
    And that we should wait a while.

Meanwhile we felt near confident
    That justice would be done
And the case of every resident
    By reason would be won.

(Eight Weeks Later)

Guess what! We've won the cause!
   The Ruling made it clear;
The Committee of Adjustment
   Must to policy adhere.

As a group we sighed relief
   Collected cash to pay the fee
Its worth that extra effort
   To maintain integrity.

Mary Comes Aboard
A Bright Day for Venture Capital (VC)

"Can we change the subject shortly?"
   I ask with patient smile.
She looked at me suspiciously
   But saw no sign of guile.

She was asking simple questions
   On VC and its state.
It must have been the seventies
   The field scarce out the gate.

"There's a man in Boston City
   By the name of Stanley Pratt.
He'd like to bring his services;
   In Canada toss his hat.

Venture Economics
   Is his company's name.
The upside's quite impressive
   Would you like to join his game?"

149

When she'd finished all her questions
   And tidied up her book,
She looked at me mysteriously
   And left with thoughtful look.

Then the two they met together
   And agreed a mutual target;
Mary opened up their office
   To serve this northern market.

When hardly two years later
   A Fund of Funds Stan started
The VC team ran out of steam
   Soon after he departed.

Then Mary joined two others
   To help steer the U.S. team.
In two years they'd fixed the problems
   And she renewed her dream.

She owned the Canuck flagship
   And high she set her sights
And the source of venture data
   Reached new and greater heights.

The rest is recent history
   That you know more than I.
When Mary takes a challenge
   She reaches for the sky.

She will always be remembered
   For her leadership and style
Ready, cheerful, able
   To go that extra mile.

And as for me, I must admit,
  I like to take some glory
For persuading our dear Mary
  To record the VC story.

The Integration of Immigration
Part I

I looked along the line of legs
And everyone was clad in jeans.
It was at the oculist I saw this sight;
They are all the same it seems.

But as I scan from floor to face
I see they are not similar.
In fact by surprise I'm taken
There's not a one familiar.

There's white and black; all shades between.
There's hair that's straight or crinkled;
There's narrow eyes, and those quite round;
All types between are sprinkled.

I know it's not my eyes that tell
This strangest tale of mixture
"Your eyes aren't bad", the doctor said,
"But your glasses are a fixture".

Then dawns on me the simple truth
It's in Canada I'm living
And everyone is welcome here -
Refuge to all the world we're giving.

A funny thing; it seems to work.
But will there come a year
When all this worldwide melting pot
Comes to the point of curdling fear?

Perhaps some caution, e'en restraint
Might be worth a thought or two.
If too far the system's stretched
Might we not unstick the glue?

Let's keep the national dream, intact
And protect our native land,
To our generous streak let's add
A sound, perhaps restraining, hand.

The Integration of Immigration
Part II

To welcome to this splendid land
All who need a place to live,
Is fine and dandy for a while;
We have, you see, the space to give.

But when all who come from overseas
Do in our cities cluster
There'll come a time, just wait and see,
When patience we will need to muster.

Tensions will surely come to boil;
Neighbourhoods will clash with fear,
Because we make no effort now
To integrate those coming here.

Let's slow the process, take a pause,
Cement our Nation's psyche,
Before we cause our dream to crash
And our land that once was mighty.

Perhaps not all who join us here
Should in big cities stay,
But for say for five years or so
In small towns should earn their way.

By surprise do not be taken
If many who fan out this way
Do in those towns so integrate
They in such diverse places stay.

Thus we might just integrate
Those we welcome to our land;
And as a strong but diverse team
So build our Nation strand by strand.

Part VI – Limericks and Other Ditties

Limerickosis

I suffer from Limerickosis
I guess its one up from necrosis
    My belly's all fired
    My brain is all wired
And it sure beats liver cirrhosis.

* * *

I must take rare medication
That causes this strange dedication
    To the limerical format
    I've become like a doormat
Rhyming without hesitation.

* * *

I have a disease called "the rhymes"
That affects the mind at odd times
    At best I make verse
    At times somewhat worse.
Why question my mind's paradigm?

A Federal Minister

I once knew a Federal Minister
Whose motives were good, never sinister.
    My friends said to me,
    "That never could be"
"The trick is in how you administer."

Some Lad

I know a lad who wasn't all bad
Though his commitment was off quite a tad
      But with humour outrageous
      He would always upstage us
And never got labelled a cad.

Farewell to David McDonough
(of SITREP)

There was a young man called McDonough
Whose editing skills were a stunner.
      On content and grammar
      He used a firm hammer,
Making Sitrep a national front-runner.

Emily's Duo

I know of a girl who's Emilian
Whose talents are truly chameleon!
      She's a mum, she can teach
      For the stars she can reach
And her knowledge is Aristotelian.

*   *   *

We have a great daughter called Emily
Who exudes a warmness quite heavenly
      But at times her sharp wit
      Can hurt quite a bit
Make hearts turn to stone all too readily.

Trip to the Loo

When Heather got locked in the loo,
She didn't know what she should do.
    So she waited and waited
    With breath that was bated
Till her sister raised Hullabaloo!

Ghislain

Ghislain is a teacher with flair,
For his students he's always right there;
    Though the length of his locks
    Causes ripples of shocks
You don't judge the man by his hair.

Our Man Howard

I know of man called Howard
A hero of squash, and no coward;
    On the courts he's a whiz
    Who makes the ball sizz
Leaves opponents in corners quite cowered.

Brenda the Wondrous Advisor

An investment advisor named Brenda
Of assets is a mighty defender;
    She was ever quite near
    To calm your worst fear
Ensuring no need of a lender.

Jen

We have a young tenant called Jen
Whom we're happy to have as a friend;
    But she lives near the roof,
    And keeps quite aloof,
So we see her just now and then.

Mia

When a war weary maiden named Mia
Saw Phil on his tank drawing nearer
    With love she was smitten
    This helpless young kitten
And it's lasted for fifty long years.

Ellen-Mary

A lady who is named Ellen-Mary
Has the charms of an elf and a fairy.
    When hitched up with Fraser
    They're sharp as a razor,
A combo that's really quite scary.

Robin

There once was a man called Robin
With the wealthy was always hob-knobbing
    When it came to fund raising
    He was really amazing
Because gifts from the rich aren't like robbing.

Kittie and her Hair

There once was a woman named Kittie
Whose hair was amazingly pretty;

But the kinks in her hair
Caused Kittie despair
So she smoothed them all out – what a pity!

Another Ditty on Kittie

There once was a lady called Kittie
Who ignored all advice, what a pity!
When the chips were all down
She said with a frown
I'd rather be bright than be pretty.

Duncan

There was a young man named Duncan
Whose smile shone more than the sun can
His charms were so forceful
And his wiles so resourceful
His body was all hickies and sun-tan.

Branksome Angst

There once was a girl from Branksome
Who usually looked very handsome
When she started to play
With a boy who was gay
Dad said, "But I long for a grandson!"

* * *

There once was a girl from Branksome
Long in leg and quite handsome;
    When I led her astray
    She said, "Nay, Nay, Nay!
My Father would hold you for ransom"

To The Bjarnson's

There once was a girl from Iceland,
Who was casting around for a nice man.
    When her eyes fell on Giorg
    She jumped over the fiord
And said, "For ever and ever, you're my man"!

A Broker Called Comeau

I know a young man called Comeau
Whose advice is scarcely pro bono;
    But his picks in the market
    Are so often on target
His clients call Comeau their hero.

Ben

I know a young man called Ben
Who avoids all voodoo and zen;
    He relies on his mind
    Most solutions to find
With results nearing ten out of ten.

Laura

I know a young teacher called Laura
Who exudes the most elegant aura;

Whether teaching teen boys
Or just calming youth's noise
You can be sure she'll produce the top scorer.

Amy

We have a young niece named Amy
Whose fantasies are few, never zany;
    With her talents prodigious
    She'll find roles prestigious,
Adding poise to a mind that's so brainy.

The Triumphant Trio

Mathieu

Mathieu was a lad tall and strong
Whose dad believed his son did no wrong;
    Imagine his surprise
    When in front of his eyes
Mathieu beat his two sisters with a thong!

Marie-Claire

There was a young lady called Claire
Who had the most beautiful hair;
    She could dance like a dream,
    Causing her siblings to scream;
 "Marie-Claire", they'd say, "wasn't fair."

Vivi

Vivi was vivacious and cuddly
Though at times her thinking was muddly;
    Played the smartest of jokes
    On a variety of folks
But they all thought her fun and quite fuddly.

Bob on the Job

Our mailman is known as Bob
He's the best of the best at his job.
    There's no-one who's better
    At delivering a letter
And having a friendly hobnob.

Our Friend Jack

We have an old friend called Jack
Whose skills are matched by his tact;
    In southern clime clinic
    Or health centre Rabbinic
Jack has the knack your health to bring back.

To Penny

I know of a lady called Penny
Whose talents are varied and many;
    She'll advise her big clients
    On disclosure and compliance
Turn a handful of shareholders into many!

Those Crazy Critters

There once was a naughty young rabbit
Who had an annoying bad habit
    He would nibble potatoes
    And demolish tomatoes
Then run fast so we couldn't quite nab it.
    *   *   *

A hawk who is known as a red-tail
Once told me this horrible bed-tale
    He'd dive from a tree
    Nab a poor chickadee
Then gulp it down on a fence rail.
    *   *   *

There's a bird of prey called a shrike
Whose victims he nabs with one strike
    Then adds to their misery
    More insult to injury
As his prey he impales on a spike.

To Cousin Mary

We got your message, Cousin,
Facsimile most welcome.
Your rhymes are dime a dozen,
Your style is never humdrum.

Now have some rest, I pray you,
The morn's a working day.
Make sure your clients yield you
A mark-up on your pay.

Oh, The Rewards!

I had a girl from private school
On the backseat of my car
When we were through she said boo-hoo
I'm going to tell my Pa!

So there we sat and had a chat
About careers and such-like.
When we were done, he said, "My son,
I've a job for you you'd much like!"

Border Banter

I may be a sentry
But there's no bar to entry
If you swear by your life
To seek peace and not strife.

Bull

Many parts of a bull are exposed to the cold
Its ears and its nose inter alia;
But most vulnerable by far of all the bull's parts
Are its generous, stupendulous genitalia.

Debt's Despair

The debt has stretched
Beyond our means.
The chance of pay-back
Less now it seems
Than riding camels
Through needle's eye
Or catching bats
In the evening sky.

Aging

I'm not enabled
And not ennobled
In fact I'm hobbled
Inclined to wobble
I'm hardly able
To clear the table
'cause I'm doddery old
No longer bold
A wispy shadow
Of my former self.
Let's face it, man,
I'm on the shelf!

Virtual

I'm a virtual virtuoso!
From reality I shrink.
I'd rather play in cyberspace;
It's easier than to think.

Dealing with the Cringe

Cringe no more
Just take the floor;
Or write a letter
And feel much better.

The Sulk

Don't blame me
Don't praise me
Just leave me alone.

Don't hurt me
Don't help me
Just let me go home.

The Apron Strings

Yes, you're my mother,
And a good one, I know,
But can't you just see that
It's time to let go!

Part VII– The Business of Business

The Motive

It may be just your ego,
  Or compulsive inside drive,
Or you want the world to know
  That alone you can survive.

To see your name in letters
  Or a winner to be called;
To prove you have no betters,
  Be as President installed.

It may be through frustration
  That you left the corporate fold,
To see your own creation
  In department stores be sold.

Or that time is running out
  On the plans you've had for years
Your employer to buy-out,
  And set the world upon its ears.

But now you're on your own, son,
  Forget what's in the past
Do whatever must be done
  To make that business last.

Whatever was the motive
  However weird or funny
Your primary objective
  Must now be making money.

"Bottom Line" please always think
  And din it in your crew
Or your ship will surely sink
  And your ego with it too.

The Time it Takes

If you think it's going to take you
    A year to make a dime
I've got news my friend to tell you
    So listen to this rhyme.

There's a rule of thumb that's simple
    And has stood the test of years,
Ignore it at your peril
    And time will prove my fears.

Take only your worst guesses
    And multiply by three
To find the time that's needed
    To profitable be.

It's not that you are wrong, friend,
    In assumptions you have made,
Or committed any errors
    In the plans that you have laid.

It's just that it takes longer
    For the world to see and hear,
And they're looking for assurance
    Next day you'll still be here.

Imagine now, I ask you,
    In what a pickle you would be,
If you'd cash enough for one year,
    And your need was really three.

On Giving or Selling Stock

Five percent, ten percent,
   All for service rendered,
Good deal, you think, my friend,
   'Till the stock is tendered.

Equity for the future is
   And not for past reward.
If a corporate founder,
   Your stock just try to horde.

I know you have no money,
   But better that you borrow
Than to advisors give
   Some slices of tomorrow.

If you take in others,
   See they pay for theirs;
If they want to leave you
   Have a "buy-back" on their shares.

Finding a Partner

When starting on a project
   On which your heart is set,
Address, I pray, the subject
   Which founders oft forget.

Can you really hope to make it
   Alone against the rest,
When competitors will take it
   A test for what is best?

Better, friend, be armed with
    A trusty founder – co;
When cold fears alarmed with,
    He'll support you as you go.

But remember that its sounder
    To find a different skill,
When seeking a co-founder;
    All else is over-kill.

What worse for opening starter
    Than a duplicate of you.
With a complementary partner
    You'd equal more than two.

So remember, please, this adage,
    As on your way you go
And turn to your advantage
    The limits that you know.

Refrain

Optimist, pessimist, extrovert or in-,
High shooter, low shooter, cheerful or grim,
When you need a partner, don't your likeness seek,
Look for the opposite and so the balance keep.

Marketer, accountant, humble or a snob,
High technological, traditional or mod,
Seek another temperament and a different skill
To test your "better" judgement and your stubborn will.

Better that together you the best route choose,
Than that in the market you your future lose.
Better with a partner you the profits share
Than alone the losses and the hurt you cannot bear.

Dealing With Your Banker

When dealing with your banker,
It is better to be franker.

Never hide with good the worse,
Or he'll tighten up his purse.

Be the first to tell bad news,
Or he'll hear through others' views.

It will help your loan be bigger
If you give him fact and figure.

When you say your loan you'll pay
Keep your promise to the day.

Hold these tenets to the letter
And your banking should get better.

If results do not prove it so,
To another banker go.

The Approach
(To Sources of Capital)

"Do it early", said the accountant,
And you waited much too long.
How can a source of capital
Assess you, weak or strong,
When the bank is pushing harder
And your payables are long?
Instead of endless stalling
It might be worth recalling
If you wait till you're insolvent
It's even harder to be confident.

"Make it pretty", said the printer
And you got it all dressed up
But the figures didn't tally,
Your proforma's all messed up.
What's the use of spending money
On a decorated shell,
When its only cold hard facts
And figures that do tell.
When I see a glossy brochure
I get a feeling: insecure.
If it's in need of such a jacket;
Then what's hidden in the packet?

"Let me introduce you",
Said the lawyer to his friend.
To some important people
He took him hand in hand.
And the lawyer did the talking
While his friend did silent stand.

When each meeting was completed
And on their way they ran,
Each individual wondered,
What he knew of this new man.
They knew their friend most talkative;
Then it hit them with a curve,
They knew nothing of the owner –
Whether backing he'd deserve.

The moral of this fable is;
Let him take you through the door
But then you do the talking -
It's in you they must feel sure.

"We'll shop", said the finder
And you knocked on every door
Little thinking that the prospect
Wondered where you'd been before.

Better than to scatter
Your approach on fronts too broad,
Try being more selective
To strike a likely chord.

The Cash Flow Budget

I heard it said
I'd soon be dead
If I didn't do a cash-flow.

Even the bank
Was more than frank
In insisting on more figures.

So off I went;
Much time was spent
In briefing my accountant.

While I was there
He did prepare
Projections most impressive.

So back I ran
To the banker man
To show him my proformas.

When he asked me why
This was low or high
I couldn't find the answer.

So with fallen crest
I left him, lest,
He embarrassed me much further.

As time went by
I thought I'd try
To understand those figures.

So I up and then
Went to my den
To spend some lonely evenings.

And then one night
A ray of light
Began to dawn within me.

I locked the door
And worked some more
And by jove I understood them.

I assumptions made
On plans I'd laid
And redid those cursed figures.

Then again I ran
To the banker man
And with confidence I showed him.

With little trouble
My line did double
As facts aligned with budgets.

Now I promise you
I'll always do
My company's projections.

I alone can say
What must go or stay,
What's a reasonable assumption.

My own cash-low
I'll always know
And I'll never be without it.

The Comfort Stage

Some time you've been in business
   And things seem nice and cosy
Competitors are lazy
   And your reputation's rosy

The market's undemanding,
   Your customers well known;
Suppliers like your golf game,
   And your balance sheet has grown.

Beware, my friend, I say
   Of an undermining trend
To slide into complacence
   Which will hurt you in the end

It's really just an attitude
   We call it "comfort stage"
To which the owner lapses
   Most oft in middle age.

In years of business upsurge
   You quite profitable will be;
When downturns hurt the others,
   You still comfortable can be.

But think my friend what happens
    When a heart attack you have,
Or want for any reason
    To on business turn your back.

Who wants to buy your company
    With no managers but you?
Remember, friend, the good ones left
    When there wasn't room for two.

And what value will they place?
    What price prepared to pay
For a no growth situation
    Which has seen a better day?

So if you feel them coming
    Fight off those slothful ways.
Work harder for a short time
    Sell your life's work while it pays.

Preparing the Company for Sale

When preparing your own company
    To be a corporate bride
Don't forget potential suitors
    Have no interest in your pride

In the years of preparation
    Please put horse before the carriage
Don't pump up non-essentials
    In your haste to make a marriage.

A clean history of sound growth
    Will stand you in better stead

Plus second level management
 To succeed you at its head.

Don't try to fudge the figures,
 They won't stand the light of day.
And if he thinks you're cheating
 He'll surely walk away.

In trying to find a value
 You always more should get
Based on your corporate earnings
 Than on its assets set.

If this is not the case
 You really should be sorry;
You'd have better been in bonds
 Without the years of worry.

When they're looking at the earnings
 Some adjustments may be made,
For personal expenses,
 And the bonus you were paid.

And if you come to terms, friend,
 Have counsel good and wise
To document the details
 And put dots on all the "i's".

If a contract they you offer
 For five years to run the show,
Don't treat it as an insult
 If in two they let you go.

On the method get advice;
   Whether assets or of shares
Is in your better interest,
   And which is more in theirs.

And finally remember
   When you're looking for a deal
Its worth more by far to someone
   Who for your business has a feel.

So look to your suppliers
   Or those in markets near
And even your competitors
   Who have looked on you with fear.

Do not be in a hurry
   Your company to sell;
A better time time to do it
   Is when it's doing well.

The Entrepreneurial Condition

There once was a company owner
Who committed the classical boner
   Tasks big or small
   Himself he did all
With the results he is sill just a loner.

* * *

There was a store clerk called Gore
Whose job was a bit of a bore;
   To assuage his ambition
   He set up competition
And became a slave to his store evermore.

* * *

There was a young man called Beadle
Who could walk through the eye of a needle.
    His feat turned to profit
    When he hired Miss Moffat
The cash from the masses to wheedle.

Inventors

There once was a man named Neal
Who tried reinventing the wheel.
    Though the concept was sound
    The result was still round
And the product lacked market appeal.

* * *

A designer became a great hero
When he created a mechanical Nero.
    On a dime it would turn
    And laugh to see Rome burn,
But its return on investment was zero.

Management Skills

When Jack knew every task how to do,
He hired others to do what he knew
    With the time he thus found
    He made plans good and sound;
Now his company's among the top few.

* * *

Quality Control

Young Bart made a treatment for hair
The answer to a young lady's prayer.
　　　　But sadly for Bart
　　　　It made their eyes smart,
And repeat orders just simply weren't there.

The Disillusioned Corporate Manager

To a manager who was surely named Moore
Corporate life became much of a bore.
　　　　With his name on a plate
　　　　He began the long wait
For customers to come to his door.

The point of this moral you see
Is that power deceitful can be;
　　　　When down from this throne
　　　　And left on his own
Moore was no "more" than you or just me.

Part VIII – In Memoriam

In Memory of John Cameron
For Ann, Doug, Barbara and Stephen

They came from every inlet,
    They came from every bay,
They came to say a last farewell
    On Cameron's farewell day.

They filled the Galbraith cottage
    With hymns and stories told
Of good times shared together
    With friends both young and old.

They remembered smooth and rough times;
    Remembered summers past;
Relived the fireside chatter
    To hold those memories fast.

They drank their gin and tonics;
    They held their glasses high,
They knew John Cameron's spirit
    Had a twinkle in its eye.

Then each took his separate leave,
    Each went his thoughtful way,
But all felt John Cameron's spirit
    Among the rocks of Go Home Bay.

Peggy 1990

Come, dear Peggy, to our garden,
    As you have since that day we met,
In summer, spring or autumn's chill,
    Early morn or when the sun is set.

Perhaps you'll bring your kneeling pad
    Nor leave behind your garden gloves
For hands so gentle yet so strong -
    Come listen to the mourning doves.

Still guide us through this flowery maze
    Of contrasts, scents and elegance;
And hand in hand let's sit and gaze
    On nature's grand beneficence.

You know them all; Forget-Me-Nots,
    Tall Hibiscus, pink and white,
The scented presence of your Phlox
    And Philadelphus' musk at night.

You know us all; Chrysanthemum,
    Or stately Tulip, Daffodil,
Primrose, Clematis, Alyssum
    Whose scent and colour gaily spill.

We are the flowers of your garden
    Some old, some young, some fame will shun;
Those who flourish when summer's gone;
    Or those who seek bright rays of sun.

We need you in our garden still,
    We need your firm, but loving care;
We need your smile upon us all;
    We need to know that you are here.

We know you're here, we feel you now;
    We are the garden where you stood;
Just stay and smile on all of us
    And say to us those words, "That's Good!"

David Hughson

David, David,
Where are you now?

They tell me you're on a trip
Perhaps up the shore of Georgian Bay,
Among the pines and restless spray;
Or are you in Bermuda's balm
Basking in its scented charm?
Or are you still among your friends
With flags and boats and odds and ends?
Or Fireman's Frolic or Council meeting
Softly speaking, always greeting?

We miss you, David,
We know you're here.
But we can't touch you
Except with tears.

Part IX – One (and two) Liners
Philosophical and Business

One (and two) Liners: Philosophical

To be right at the wrong time, is to be wrong

If in doubt, say no

You can't make time but you can make better use
of it

Logic can help make a decision, timing can make
it a good one

Is the glass half full or the glass half empty?
The pessimist's drought
Is the optimist's plenty.

The optimist's smile
Beats the pessimist's guile

Random access = Hi-tech greed

And when they close the book
Let them say of me,
He gave more than he took.

One thing is to mouth it, another is to mean it.

Does it resonate or detonate?

Never say, "If only I!"
Never say, "Oh why, oh why?"

You may know where he's coming from;
But do you know where he's going to?

Old age – feeling a few cogs in the old gear shift.

Worry is a parental prerogative.

The best advice to help people;
Ask the right questions – of themselves and of
others.

Casualness may bring on casualty.

The age of enlightenment
Has given way
To the age of entitlement.

I saw my reflection
But it went
In the other direction.

Does it freeze or fuse
Or simply blow the mind?

Mind over matter
Time over chatter.

Rein in your arrogant greed;
Don't mistake a want for a need.

American Solution to Y2K problem; the Clinton
computer; 8" hard drive, with no memory.

One (and two) Liners: Business

Anyone can trade dollars; only good managers make them.

All owners are optimists; successful owners are realists.

Marginal accounting has produced many sub-marginal decisions.

Beware economics of scale, they rarely materialize.

The purpose of owning a company is to run it, not let it run you.

If you can't take it with you, why not get out while you can still enjoy the proceeds.

Helping people help themselves is good business.

Only governments help people despite themselves.

It takes courage to start a business; it takes a lot more to keep it going.

The customers know best – ask them.

Manage for a rainy day; tomorrow may be one.

To manage is to get things done through people.

Remove dead wood; rot is contagious.

To own a business is a good feeling; to run a profitable one is a great achievement.

Write it down, or it may not exist.

The Comfort Stage is only comfortable until you want to sell.

If you've reached a plateau, beware; the slide down is easier than the climb up – you won't even notice it.

If necessity is the mother of invention, competition is its father.

There are a hundred good reasons to get into business; but only one to stay – profit.

Never promise more than you can deliver.

To be successful, know which 20% of your products produce 80% of the profit.

It takes years to build a reputation, one mistake to lose it.

One introduction is worth three cold calls.

There's always a niche in a market too awkward for the big company to service; find it and fill it.

(On inventory); If it doesn't move, kick it out.

Don't reward sales people for sales, reward them for profitable sales.

Equity is a share in the future – keep it in the hands of those who will influence the future.

Beware of giving equity to employees – better to make them pay for it, even at a favourable price on easy terms.

An employee can only help you solve a problem if he knows what it is.

To start into a manufacturing operation with less than a 30% gross margin is to court disaster.

Competition may ignore you when you have 5% of a market; watch out when you reach 15%.

It is easier to lower prices than to raise them.

Beware of relying too heavily on one supplier – he may let you down.

Call your lawyer before, not after, you make a deal.

To be a good leader is different from being a good manager.

Printed in the United States
94986LV00001B/121-255/A